ESSAYS ON PHILOSOPHICAL METHOD

New Studies in Practical Philosophy

General Editor: W. D. Hudson

The point of view of this series is that
of contemporary analytical philosophy.
Each study will deal with an aspect of
moral philosophy. Particular attention
will be paid to the logic of moral discourse,
and the practical problems of morality.
The relationship between morality and
other 'universes of discourse', such as art
and science, will also be explored.

Published:

R. M. Hare, *Practical Inferences*
R. M. Hare, *Essays on Philosophical Method*

Among the titles in preparation are:
R. M. Hare, *Essays on the Moral Concepts*
R. M. Hare, *Applications of Moral Philosophy*

ESSAYS ON PHILOSOPHICAL METHOD

R. M. HARE

White's Professor of Moral Philosophy
in the University of Oxford

UNIVERSITY OF CALIFORNIA PRESS

Berkeley and Los Angeles 1972

UNIVERSITY OF CALIFORNIA PRESS

Berkeley and Los Angeles, California

ISBN: 0–520–02178–9

Library of Congress Catalog Card Number: 76–182286

© R. M. Hare 1971 except where stated

Printed in Great Britain

Contents

Acknowledgements

P. Schilpp (ed.), *The Philosophy of C. D. Broad*, Tudor Publishing Co., New York, 1959. *Mind*, LXIX, N.S., no. 274, 1960. *Journal of Philosophy*, LIV, 1957. *Ratio*, II, no. 2, 1960. Mario Bunge (ed.), *The Critical Approach: Essays in Honor of Karl Popper*, Free Press of Glencoe, Illinois, 1964. Renford Bambrough (ed.), *New Essays on Plato and Aristotle*, Routledge & Kegan Paul, London, 1964.

Editor's Foreword

Philosophy is a discipline which has a long history yet is as lively now as it has ever been. What is true of the subject as a whole is true in particular of that branch of it which is called ethics or moral philosophy. In this volume one of the foremost of modern philosophers sets his reflections on philosophical method within the context of both classical and contemporary philosophy.

Professor Hare is the leading exponent of that type of ethical theory known as prescriptivism. The two books in which he expounds it, *The Language of Morals* (1952) and *Freedom and Reason* (1963), have had a wide influence and occasioned heated agreement and disagreement. The most interesting controversy among moral philosophers at the present time is between those who consider Hare's views to be substantially correct and those who advance against him a type of theory which is coming to be known as descriptivism. The present volume is one of four which together present a comprehensive collection of Hare's writings throughout his professional career. They form a background to the views expressed in his two books and acquaintance with their contents is essential for anyone who wishes to understand prescriptivism. The present volume, like each of the other three, contains some papers which have not previously been published. Of those papers which are reprinted from other journals or collections, some are no longer easily accessible elsewhere.

W. D. HUDSON

University of Exeter

Preface

This volume is the second of a set in which I am collecting the more considerable of my published papers, together with some hitherto unpublished work. I have included in it a number of pieces which seemed to fit well together, though written for many different purposes and occasions. They all treat of various aspects of the questions, 'What can philosophy (and in particular moral philosophy) achieve ?', and 'How does (or how should) it set about achieving it ?' Though several of them have historical-sounding titles, their point is not merely historical.

In the first volume of the set, *Practical Inferences*, I included a bibliography of my published writings, in which the contents of the other volumes can be discovered. In preparing the papers for the present volume I have kept alterations to the minimum that was editorially necessary; the fourth essay has, however, been restored, more or less, to the state it was in before the original publishers (not having commented on the typescript) 'improved' it too radically for complete remedy at the proof stage.

The sixth piece, which has not appeared before, was given as my inaugural lecture at Oxford, and is printed in the form it would have had if I had followed the usual uneconomic and inconvenient practice of publishing it separately. The seventh piece is new. The original publishers of the rest are identified in the Acknowledgements; I am grateful to them for giving their permission where necessary. I must also, as before, express my sincere thanks to the General Editor and publishers of the present series for their moral and material support in a venture on which I would otherwise have lacked the effrontery to embark.

R. M. HARE

Corpus Christi College,
Oxford
1970

1 Broad's Approach to Moral Philosophy

When, as a student beginning moral philosophy, I first read *Five Types of Ethical Theory* (then as now one of the most-used textbooks in the subject), I remember being scandalised, as were many of my contemporaries, by its concluding passage:

> We can no more learn to act rightly by appealing to the ethical theory of right action than we can play golf well by appealing to the mathematical theory of the flight of the golf-ball. The interest of ethics is thus almost wholly theoretical, as is the interest of the mathematical theory of golf or of billiards. And yet it may have a certain slight practical application. It may lead us to look out for certain systematic faults which we should not otherwise have suspected; and, once we are on the look out for them, we may learn to correct them. But in the main the old saying is true: *Non in dialectica complacuit Deo salvum facere populum suum*. Not that this is any objection to dialectic. For salvation is not everything; and to try to understand in outline what one solves *ambulando* and in detail is quite good fun for those people who like that sort of thing.[1]

We had just returned from a war during which we had been personally confronted with a number of moral questions which did not admit of an easy answer. Many of us hoped that philosophy might be of assistance to us in answering these questions. Indeed, that was what made us study this subject, rather than others more obviously relevant to practical problems. We were no doubt wrong to object to Broad just because his idea of fun differed from our own. But could it be that when people found the money to pay the stipends of philosophical professors,

From *The Philosophy of C. D. Broad*, ed. P. Schilpp, Tudor Publishing Company, (New York, 1959).

[1] *FTET*, p. 285.

their main object was to enable these professors to amuse themselves?

The dislike of a priggish undergraduate for his prescribed reading may seem a matter of no importance; yet I have mentioned it because it is one of the purposes of this paper to show how unjust, in many respects, this criticism was. It was founded upon ignorance – ignorance of both the historical and the logical reasons which had led Broad to write in this way. It is worth while to examine these reasons; for moral philosophers have often found themselves subjected to criticism of this sort, especially in the present century. The criticism takes many forms, but the cause of the dissatisfaction is usually the same. I shall endeavour to show that the tendency in modern ethics which has provoked this dissatisfaction owes its origin to the work of the intuitionist school, of which Broad is an able representative. This fact should be obvious to anyone who has understood what has been happening in ethics during the past fifty years; but it is worth while to draw attention to it, since it is commonly thought that more recent writers are to blame for the tendency.

A proper treatment of the problem requires a survey of the development of philosophers' views on the point at issue during the first half of this century, together with an attempt to set the question in its true light. Since both these tasks will take me some distance away from Broad's own writings, I wish to explain that my object in this paper is not directly to discuss (let alone to criticise) what little he has written about the scope of moral philosophy. It might indeed be said that on this, as on other questions, Broad has been very chary of expounding his own views; his fame rests on his admirably clear discussion and criticism of the views of others. But since his writings give evidence of a consistent attitude to this question; and since the attitude is a widely-held one and the question itself of fundamental importance, this seems too good an opportunity to miss of raising the question, and thus compelling Broad, in his reply, to say, more fully than he has done, what he thinks about it.

In a volume devoted to Broad's philosophy, a historical survey of recent developments might appropriately have started with Sidgwick; but for reasons of space I shall not go so far back. I shall start with Moore. I do not know whether, when Moore wrote 'The direct object of ethics is knowledge and not practice', he was consciously controverting Aristotle's equally famous remark on the same subject;[1] but it may fairly be said that the publication of *Principia Ethica* in 1903 marks a great break with tradition, and the beginning of a new way of thinking about this question – as about so many others. This is not to say that the distinction which Moore made between ethical theory and moral judgement had not been made before in ethics; it was made, in different words, by Socrates.[2] But it owes to Moore its prominence in recent ethics. The distinction is that between two questions, both of which might be expressed by the words 'What is good?' This question might, says Moore, be taken as meaning 'What (sorts of) things are good?'; but it might be taken as meaning 'How is "good" to be defined?'[3] And though Moore included under the name 'ethics' attempts to answer both these questions, he regarded the latter question as prior and treated it in the first half of his book; and it was his attempt to answer it (an attempt whose results were startlingly negative) which has provided the stimulus to nearly every important development in ethics from that day to this.

It has recently been suggested by Dr Raphael[4] that, while recent moral philosophers have, with a one-sidedness which he condemns, concentrated on the question which Moore treated first in his book, the second half of the book was what counted most 'outside the circle of professional philosophers'. Lord Keynes and the Bloomsbury group are instanced in support of this contention. But what inspired Keynes and his friends were not just Moore's opinions about what things were good, treated simply as opinions – as such they were not perhaps strikingly

[1] G. E. Moore, *Principia Ethica*, p. 20; Aristotle, *Eth. Nic.*, 1103 b27. It now (1971) seems to me that the usual interpretation of this passage, which is assumed in the text, is mistaken. It means, rather, 'For we are enquiring what goodness is, not for the (mere) sake of knowing it, but in order that we may (by using this knowledge) become good'. For Aristotle, as for Moore, the *direct* object of ethics was knowledge, its ultimate object practice. This interpretation is neatly supported by the fact that, one and a half pages further on, he resumes his enquiry in the identical terms: 'After these preliminaries, we have to enquire what goodness is.'

[2] See, for example, Plato, *Euthyphro*, 6 d.

[3] Moore, op. cit., pp. 3–5.

[4] In an unpublished paper, 'Recent Oxford Contributions to Ethics', read to the Oxford colloquium on Contemporary British Philosophy, 1955.

distinctive. It is quite clear from Keynes's *Memoirs* that the reason why Moore was treated as a prophet was not merely that he propounded certain value-judgements (though these value-judgements *did* inspire them), but also that he had important new things to say about the nature of value-judgements and the way they are made. And Moore's doctrine about method was the direct outcome of his refutation of naturalism.[1]

As Keynes's biographer puts it,

> The doctrine of indefinability has the consequence that decisions about what is good depend on direct intuition in each particular case. The interpretation given in Oxford to this consequence was widely different from that in Cambridge. In Oxford – no doubt owing partly to the special attention paid to Aristotle's *Ethics* – great reliance was placed on what may be called traditional morality, embodying the intuitions of wise men through the ages. In Cambridge the doctrine of intuition was interpreted – anyhow by those disciples who were to be for many years the intimate intellectual companions of Keynes – as giving fairly complete licence to judge all things anew.[2]

'How did we know (says Keynes himself) what states of mind were good? This was a matter of direct inspection, or direct unanalysable intuition about which it was useless and impossible to argue.'[3] Yet Keynes and his friends *did* argue; and their arguments were of a sort which is in one respect strikingly similar to those employed in the most recent philosophical discussions in Oxford about ethical questions. Moore's disciples used the methods of linguistic analysis (of which Moore has a good claim to be called the modern inventor) in order to clarify evaluative questions. This was the only form argument *could* take, since once the issues were clarified, there was no further place for argument. 'We spent our time (says Keynes) trying to discover *precisely what* questions we were asking, confident in the faith that, if only we could ask precise questions, everyone

---

[1] I shall use the term 'naturalism' to cover any theory which is refutable by the argument which Moore used, or a recognisable reformulation of that argument: that is, roughly, any theory which treats an evaluative expression as equivalent to a descriptive expression. I have given my own reformulation of Moore's argument in *Language of Morals*, chap. 5.

[2] R. F. Harrod, *Life of J. M. Keynes*, p. 77.

[3] Keynes, *Two Memoirs*, p. 84.

would know the answer.'[1] And of these arguments he says,
'It was a method of discovery by the instrument of impeccable
grammar and an unambiguous dictionary. "What *exactly* do
you mean ?" was the phrase most frequently on our lips.'[2] Thus,
in deciding a question of value, argument (traditionally the
province of moral philosophers) was confined to the elucidation
of terms. Once these were understood there was nothing left
to argue about; the individual had to make his own judgements
of value, and, provided that the verbal elucidation had been
done properly, individuals would not (so it was thought) disagree. It was only this pious hope which distinguished this kind
of intuitionism from the most extreme form of subjectivism –
and this should remind us that these two doctrines, superficially
so different, are not in fact very dissimilar.

Keynes also says that, preoccupied with this intoxicating
business of evaluating personal experiences under the powerful
illumination provided by the analysis of meaning, they paid
scant attention to what Moore had to say about morals, in the
narrow sense in which it means 'our attitude towards the outside
world'. 'There was one chapter in the *Principia*', he says, 'of
which we took not the slightest notice', namely the chapter
called 'Ethics in Relation to Conduct'.[3] This disrespect towards
morals led the outside world – even including D. H. Lawrence,
whose actual evaluations were not so far removed as were con-
ventional people's from those of Moore's disciples – to regard
the group with suspicion, in the same way, and for the same
reasons, as it has suspected the disciples of some later philosophers who have insisted on the distinction which Moore made
current. What, according to Keynes, repelled Lawrence was

---

[1] Op. cit., p. 89. Moore's remarks on p. 6 of *Principia Ethica* might seem to
conflict with Keynes's description of his method; he there says that his
business is not with 'proper usage, as defined by custom'. The truth is that
neither Moore nor analysts of the generation which succeeded him are tied,
as lexicographers are, to the *actual* current usage of words (though these
may guide them). Their only concern is that, however words are being used,
it should be explained how they are being used. But this is not to be taken
as a licence to evade the discussion and elucidation of problematical concepts by the subterfuge of substituting for them concepts which do not raise
the same problems; see my *Language of Morals*, pp. 91 ff. The transition
from 'words' to 'concepts' is here crucial.

[2] Op. cit., p. 88.

[3] Op. cit., p. 82; Moore, *Principia Ethica*, chap. 5.

'this thin rationalism . . . joined to libertinism and comprehensive irreverence'.[1]

The implications of the new division of moral philosophy made by Moore became very apparent nine years later, when Prichard (the first of the Oxford School of intuitionists referred to by Mr Harrod) published his famous article 'Does Moral Philosophy Rest on a Mistake?' The article concludes with the following statement:

> If we do doubt whether there is really an obligation to originate A in a situation B, the remedy lies not in any process of general thinking, but in getting face to face with a particular instance of the situation B, and then directly appreciating the obligation to originate A in that situation.[2]

By 'general thinking' Prichard seems to have meant the sort of thinking which had occupied the greater part of many books on moral philosophy up to his day. These books consisted of a number of different sorts of discussion, not always clearly distinguished by their authors;[3] Moore had pointed the way to a proper classification of these different elements in moral philosophy – a classification which, when insisted on, seemed to make certain of the elements irrelevant to certain others. A typical work of moral philosophy of the old type contains three main kinds of observation. First, there are statements of fact about how things stand in the world – in particular, statements about what sorts of actions will have what sorts of results. Secondly, we have statements about the nature of the concepts used in moral thinking, or, as a modern would put it, about the meaning or function or use of moral words. Thirdly, the books

---

[1] Op. cit., pp. 75 f, 78, 98, 103.   [2] *Moral Obligation*, p. 17.

[3] Kant's question is perhaps here pertinent: 'whether it would not be better for the whole of this learned industry if those accustomed to purvey, in accordance with the public taste, a mixture of the empirical and the rational in various proportions unknown to themselves – the self-styled "creative thinkers" as opposed to the "hair-splitters" who attend to the pure rational part – were to be warned against carrying on at once two jobs very different in their technique, each perhaps requiring a special talent and the combination of both in one person producing mere bunglers!' (*Groundwork*, iv; H. J. Paton's translation, p. 56). Kant objected not so much to the same person doing both jobs (he did himself) but to doing them 'at once'. The force of Kant's warning is not weakened by the discovery that there are, not two, but at least three jobs.

generally conclude with some statements of moral principle which are held by the author to have been established by what has gone before.

Now Hume, in a well-known passage, which Prichard echoes in this same article, had shown the impropriety of the direct passage from the first of these three kinds of statement to the third.[1] But many moral philosophers (including perhaps Hume himself) seem to have supposed that the second kind of statement could help us out of this difficulty; that discoveries about the nature of goodness, obligation, etc., could somehow provide a bridge over the gulf between factual statement and moral principle. Moore's exposure of the 'naturalistic fallacy', extended by Prichard to cover 'ought' as well as 'good', seemed to have put this approach to the subject out of court once for all. The way to settle moral problems, when all the necessary fact-finding had been done, was by intuition. The study of the moral concepts, or the attempt to analyse moral terms, did indeed need undertaking; but its results were purely negative, and its sole use was to proclaim that they were negative, in order to prevent the unwary from falling into naturalistic errors. And since both Moore and Prichard had proclaimed this in clear tones, it is not surprising that, when Broad came on the scene, there seemed to be not much scope for the traditional sort of moral philosophy – the sort which claimed to be able to reach conclusions of moral principle.

This explains very clearly the feature of Broad's book which, as an undergraduate, I found unattractive. It too consists of three elements, but they are not the same three as I mentioned above. To mention first the element which occupies least space, there are some moral observations, many of them very wise, and all expressed with admirable clarity and pungency. These are to be found scattered throughout *Five Types*. They are not, however, represented as the results of any peculiarly philosophical enquiry; in so far as Broad judges moral issues, his tendency is to judge them as a man, not as philosophy professor. This is much to his credit, and makes the judgements themselves more valuable than they might otherwise have been.[2] But the

[1] Hume, *Treatise III*, 1, i, last para.; Prichard, op. cit., p. 4.
[2] For an example of a judgement by Broad on a specific moral issue, see the devastating comparison between the personal morals of Sidgwick and Green

separation between ethical theory and moral judgement is in *FTET* almost complete.

The second element in *FTET* consists of analytical studies of the various moral concepts, together with an accurate and painstaking classification of the different theories which might be held about the meaning of moral judgements and their epistemological status. The third element consists of historical studies of particular philosophers, whose views are dissected and displayed in terms of the aforementioned classification. It is perhaps not unfair to say that only by including this valuable historical matter was Broad able to fill a book about moral philosophy – so attenuated had the subject become through the work of his predecessors.

The history of moral philosophy in the years when Broad's own thought was developing not merely explains, but in large measure justifies, his approach to the subject. For although there were ambiguities in Moore's presentation of his argument against naturalism, and although few people nowadays would accept an intuitionism of the type advocated by Prichard, yet the facts about the nature of moral discourse that led these writers to the views which I have described are indeed facts; and they do indeed render impossible of fulfilment the traditional programme of moral philosophers, that of using logical considerations, arising out of the meanings of the moral words, to get them from an 'is' to an 'ought'. And Broad, by refusing to engage in these traditional endeavours and devoting himself instead to enquiries of a historical and analytical kind, was showing himself an honest man. He has never joined the ranks of those who, not liking the effects of the distinction made by Moore, seek to blur it – a thing which it is easy enough to do if, deliberately or by reason of an ocular defect, the subject is put sufficiently out of focus. I must therefore admit that my juvenile irritation at Broad's remarks was entirely unjustified. Yet there remains with me a certain dissatisfaction, not with Broad, but with the state of the subject. Since dissatisfaction of this sort has been voiced recently in more than one quarter, it

---

in *FTET*, pp. 12 and 144. Some later papers contain very penetrating applications of ethical theory to moral problems, and perhaps indicate a change of attitude since *Five Types*. See especially the last two papers in *Ethics and the History of Philosophy*.

may not be inapposite to discuss its cause; by this means I may perhaps draw Broad himself into the debate.

It is still frequently said of present-day moral philosophy that it has become 'impoverished' by concentrating on the analysis of concepts. I take this word from a broadcast talk by Mr J. W. N. Watkins. As I have indicated, those who make this kind of attack upon recent writers do not often go back far enough in their search for whipping-boys. The distinction between the analysis of moral concepts and the actual propounding of moral judgements is implicit in the work of Moore, and its consequences are plain for all to see in the work of the intuitionist school. Yet sometimes writers, who do not like the way moral philosophy is done at the present time, attribute this distinction, and the ethical method which it suggests, to a more recent school of ethical writers, of whom Professor Ayer is the most controversial representative. To see how this accusation has come to be so misdirected is not irrelevant to the study of Broad's philosophy, since it is evident from his writings that, unlike some intuitionists who were not in the thick of the controversy at Cambridge, he took the new developments of the twenties and thirties seriously enough to understand them; and, although he did not accept the new ideas, they had a considerable impact on his thought.[1] The predicament in which these new developments had placed the moral philosopher provides an additional explanation of Broad's attitude to the subject.

I am not well enough versed in the recent history of ethics to be able to identify with assurance the first clear statement in modern times of what came to be known as the Emotive theory. If we ignore such earlier hints as that to be found in Berkeley's *Principles*,[2] and consider only the theory as recently maintained, we can trace it back, in a clearly formulated shape, at least as far as Ogden and Richards's *Meaning of Meaning* (1923).[3] By 1925 Ramsey was able to write: 'Most of us would agree that the objectivity of good was a thing we had settled and dismissed

[1] See especially Broad's discussion in *Ar. Soc.*, XXXIV (1933–4) 249 ff. of the views of Duncan-Jones.

[2] *Principles of Human Knowledge*, Intro. § 20.

[3] See especially p. 125. The theory or something very like it was developed much earlier by certain Scandinavian philosophers, the most important of whom, Hägerström, has recently been translated by Broad. See also H. Ofstad's article in *Philosophy and Phenomenological Research*, XII (1951) 42 ff.

B

with the existence of God. Theology and Absolute Ethics are two famous subjects which we have realized to have no real objects.'[1] It is surprising, therefore, that Ayer's own *Language, Truth and Logic*, which appeared more than ten years later, created such a stir, and is still the principal butt of those who wish to attack the theory. The explanation is that the chapter in that book devoted to ethics is a masterpiece of philosophical writing, whose clarity, sharpness and earnestness could rouse even the most dogmatic from their slumbers; and that it was written in Oxford, where philosophers had been sleeping longer and more deeply, and therefore more resented being woken up.

Ayer, however, stepped so easily into the leadership of the new school in England that it is to the common criticisms of his views, and his replies to them, that we must look if we are to understand the present state of the subject. The most important thing, historically, to notice about Ayer is his enormous debt to Moore. The general debt of the emotivists to Moore, and the close relation of their views to his, has been recognised by Professor Stevenson, and half-acknowledged by Moore himself.[2] But very striking confirmations of this debt are to be found in the pages of *Language, Truth and Logic*. If Moore had not written *Principia Ethica*, any philosopher of an empiricist turn of mind who espoused, like Ayer, a verificationist theory of meaning would have been drawn irresistibly to some form of ethical naturalism, whether of a psychological kind which maintains that moral judgements are statements that the speaker, or that people in general, have certain feelings, or of some kind which holds that they are statements about non-psychological empirical fact. But Ayer had understood Moore well enough not to take either of these ways out; and the brilliantly clear statement of the impossibility of naturalism which *Language, Truth and Logic* contains is nothing but a refinement of Moore's argument.[3] Even when he turns to criticise Moore, Ayer reveals his debt to him by the seriousness with which he takes Moore's arguments; but the clearest and neatest indication of the relation between the two philosophers is in the following two passages,

[1] F. P. Ramsey, *Foundations of Mathematics*, p. 288, referred to by Ayer, *Philosophical Essays*, p. 231.

[2] *The Philosophy of G. E. Moore*, ed. P. A. Schilpp, pp. 546 f. Cf. C. L. Stevenson, *Ethics and Language*, pp. 272 f.

[3] Ayer, *Language, Truth and Logic*, 2nd ed., pp. 104 f.

the first from *Principia Ethica* and the second from *Language, Truth and Logic*:

> In fact, if it is not the case that 'good' denotes something simple and indefinable, only two alternatives are possible: either it is a complex, a given whole, about the correct analysis of which there may be disagreement; or else it means nothing at all, and there is no such subject as ethics.[1]

> Having upheld our theory against the only criticism which appeared to threaten it (Moore's), we may now use it to define the nature of all ethical enquiries. We find that ethical philosophy consists simply in saying that ethical concepts are pseudo-concepts and therefore unanalysable.[2]

Moore thought that he had disposed of one of the possibilities which he lists – that what 'good' denotes is a complex (naturalism); and with this conclusion Ayer agrees. Yet in the years since *Principia Ethica* Moore's own suggestion, that it was a simple indefinable non-natural quality (intuitionism), had ceased to satisfy anybody; and Moore himself has since confessed (in 1942) that 'in *Principia* I did not give any tenable explanation of what I meant by saying that "good" was not a natural property'.[3] These two possibilities excluded, only the third seemed to Ayer to be open; and he seized it with relish.

The continuity of ethics in the present century is therefore much greater than has sometimes been thought by those who looked at developments from too close quarters. The two results of Moore's work which are important for our purpose may be summed up as follows: he established that it was impossible, by studying the nature, function or analysis of moral concepts, to build a logical bridge between factual premisses and moral conclusions; and he showed that our moral judgements are the result of something which we have to do for ourselves, and which cannot be done for us or forced on us by appeal to any definition or empirical observation. Whether we call this something an intuition, as did the earlier writers, or a feeling of approval, as did the later, is a question of small relative importance, resting on a verbal distinction which nobody has ever succeeded in making clear. Intuitionists and emotivists are on the same side in this at any rate, that they make it difficult to see much direct

---

[1] Moore, op. cit., p. 15.
[2] Ayer, op. cit., p. 112. Ayer's later writings show more moderate views.
[3] *The Philosophy of G. E. Moore* (Schilpp), p. 582.

connection between ethical theory and moral judgement. Broad lies precisely on the dividing-line between these two schools – superficially so different but actually so closely related; and that is why I am doing my utmost to elicit from him, in his reply, a statement of his present views about this question.

In order to indicate some of the possible moves, it is useful to consider how Ayer has fared in answering his critics. The first criticism which was made was that his views on ethics were morally damnable, in that they were an encouragement to all who read them to stop caring about morality and live as they pleased. The accusation of libertinism was not new, as we have seen. To this Ayer's reply has always been:

> I am not saying that morals are trivial or unimportant, or that people ought not to bother with them. For this would itself be a judgment of value, which I have not made and do not wish to make. And even if I did wish to make it, it would have no logical connection with my theory. For the theory is entirely on the level of analysis; it is an attempt to show what people are doing when they make moral judgments; it is not a set of suggestions as to what moral judgments they are to make. All moral theories, intuitionist, naturalistic, objectivist, emotive, and the rest, are neutral as regards actual conduct. To speak technically, they belong to the field of meta-ethics, not ethics proper.[1]

Ayer here rebuts the charge that his theory entails depraved moral views by saying that it entails no one moral view rather than another. Ayer is quite right to claim here that this is true, not only of his own theory but of intuitionism too; in this respect, as we have seen, there is no difference between the two theories.

In using this defence, however, against the accusation that he is a corrupting moral influence, Ayer lays himself open to another attack. If ethical theories are neutral as regards actual conduct – if judgements of value can have no logical connection with such a theory – then what is the point of ethics ? This is, as I have said, a question which is frequently asked, not only about Ayer's work, but about that of other ethical writers of the present time; I have more than once been asked it myself, in a somewhat hostile spirit. It is a question which anyone must face who holds that ethics is concerned with the analysis of moral concepts.

[1] Ayer, *Philosophical Essays*, p. 245.

It might be replied to this accusation that ethics, like any branch of learning, should be pursued for its own sake. The ethical philosopher is in the same position as the pure mathematician, or the Hebrew scholar; his discoveries may turn out to have a practical use, but this ought not to be his concern. Ethics is a branch of logic, and has many points of intimate contact with other branches of that subject. It is at least *as* important to study the logic of words like 'ought' as it is to study that of words like 'all'; and since in fact the different branches of logic illuminate one another, the logician has very good reason to study *any* sort of word that interests him. Moreover, unless philosophy is going to be given up altogether, logic must surely be allowed to survive; and if logic, then the branch of logic called ethics.

This reply, however, is not much more likely to satisfy some of the attackers than is Broad's own reply that ethics is 'fun'. For not only do many people take to ethics just because they think that they will learn something which will help them in making moral decisions; they take to philosophy itself because ethics is part of philosophy, and cannot be understood without studying the whole subject. In the eyes of these people (who include many, though not all, of the great philosophers) ethics cannot be justified merely because it is part and parcel of philosophy, since the justification of philosophy itself is that its study is of value to ethics. Some people may be happy to go on sorting out philosophical perplexities without worrying about whether they are doing any service to their fellow men. But it may be doubted whether the subject would ever have got started if it had not been thought to have more relevance to men's needs than that. To this it might be retorted that chemistry would never have got started if people had not hoped to enrich themselves by turning base metals into gold; and that it is no slur on philosophy to say that the first incentive to its pursuit was a false hope of finding an alchemy that would extract evaluative conclusions from factual premisses. But chemistry has at least *become* useful; whereas it is often said that ethics has now lost whatever use it formerly had.

Be this as it may, the defence of ethics which we have been considering is not the only possible one. It may be said that ethics *clarifies* moral issues by bringing out the exact use of the words used in discussing them, and thus guarding against verbal confusions. This claim also excites a good deal of antipathy. For most people think that they know well enough how to use the moral words, until the philosopher gets at them; the philosopher, it is said, increases rather than diminishes the confusion. This kind of thing was said of Socrates when he pressed his paralysing demand for an analysis of moral concepts, and it is said today.[1] It is also said that in fact ethical philosophers have not, by analysis, succeeded in clearing up any perplexities about moral questions that really perplex people.

To this it might be replied that to feel quite clear about the use of the moral words may be a sign of the most radical confusion about them. Meno, in the dialogue bearing his name to which I have just referred, felt quite clear that he knew what virtue was; but his attempts to say *what* it was show how little he understood what sort of concept he was trying to define. Certainty about the use of moral words is often a sign of dogmatism; and the extreme kind of dogmatism is naturalism, the view that our own moral views are true in virtue of the very meanings of words. The analytical study of concepts like 'good' has at least this negative effect, that it may show people that they really have to make up their own minds about questions of value, and cannot have these questions answered for them by definition. And this is no small gain.

But few people really think that their moral problems can be solved, in the last resort, by anyone but themselves. They do not need a philosopher to tell them this. What they want the philosopher to do is to give them some assistance in solving those problems. And when it is seen that this assistance cannot take the form of showing that certain answers to the problems are true by definition, they will ask what form the assistance *is* going to take.

To this question I can only suggest the answer that has satisfied me, and ask Professor Broad whether he agrees with it. I took to moral philosophy because I was perplexed about moral problems; and I am quite satisfied that the study of the logical function of the moral words has considerably reduced my perplexity. I now know a great deal better (though I am far from knowing with clear certainty) what I am doing when I am

[1] See, for example, *Meno*, 79 e ff.

asking a moral question; and this makes it a great deal easier to answer the question. Moral issues, as anyone can observe who watches how they present themselves in real life, come to us as a confused mixture of questions of fact and questions of value, together with a large element of questions concerning the meanings of words. In the more difficult cases we cannot begin to answer these questions till we have established to which of these classes they belong. Everyday moral discussions are full of confusions between questions of fact, requiring empirical investigation, questions of definition, requiring an agreement on how to use words, and questions of value, requiring evaluative decisions. It is often not impossible to answer these various sorts of questions, once we have sorted them out; and ethics is a training in doing this.

This, however, is not the only contribution of ethics to the solution of moral problems. It has also a more positive role. For it may be that once we know what we mean by calling a question a *moral* question, we shall stop wanting to answer it in certain ways. But this I most emphatically do not mean that, as some writers have seemed to maintain, moral conclusions of substance can be derived by means of some quasi-logic from factual premises in virtue of a definition of the word 'moral'.[1] This would be nothing but a highly sophisticated form of naturalism. What I intend may be illustrated by an example. I think that it can be maintained, by means of logical considerations alone resting on the meaning of the expression 'morally wrong', that what is not morally wrong for me to do in this situation is not morally wrong for anyone to do in a similar situation. The word 'similar' is here to be taken to mean that whatever qualitative predicates can be truthfully applied to one situation can be truthfully applied to the other; and 'qualitative' is to be taken as excluding overt or implicit use of singular terms and also of evaluative terms in the predicate. This statement is not sufficiently precise, but it will do for my present purpose.[2] Now the statement that I have just made is not a

---

[1] For a criticism of a theory of this sort, see my review of Professor Toulmin's *Reason in Ethics* in *Philosophical Quarterly*, 1 (1951) 372 ff.

[2] I have tried to state this thesis more clearly, and to defend it, in *Ar. Soc.*, LV (1954–5) 297 ff. (reprinted in my *Essays on The Moral Concepts* (forthcoming)); and I have given an example of the practical effect of the thesis in *The Listener*, LIV (1955) 651 f.; see also the essay 'Peace', in my *Applications of Moral Philosophy* (forthcoming), and *Freedom and Reason*.

statement of substance; it is logically compatible with absolutely any single act being either wrong, or not wrong. No synthetic judgement follows from the statement; if true, it is analytically so in virtue of the meaning of the words 'morally wrong'. But if I am asking whether a certain act which I am contemplating is morally wrong or not, this analytic statement may be of considerable import to me. For if I realise that the judgement, that it is not morally wrong for *me* to do this act to a certain man, entails the judgement that it would not be wrong for someone else to do a similar act to me, were the situation similar, then I may feel disinclined to say that it is not morally wrong; I may feel inclined, rather, to say that it *is* morally wrong. And so I may eliminate from the alternatives offered to my choice a possibility that was previously open.

I say 'I may feel inclined'. Whether I *do* feel inclined will depend on two conditions. The first is that I have sufficient imagination to visualise myself in the position of the other man. The second is that I am averse to suffering that experience which I imagine myself suffering, were I in the other man's place. So we have, in all, three conditions which determine my inclination to say that a certain act would be wrong. The first is, that I should understand the word 'wrong' sufficiently to know that its use is governed by the principle which I enunciated in the preceding paragraph. The second is, that I should have sufficient imagination. The third is, that I should have certain likes and dislikes of certain experiences. It is to be noticed that none of these conditions presupposes any previous moral opinions of substance on my part; so that the argument which I have used does not rely upon any suppressed moral premises. It is also to be remarked that, though I have stated these distinctions in terms which have a psychological ring, an exact statement of them would reveal my contentions to be analytic.

Broad, in discussing Kant, deals with this question in greater detail than I have had the space to do.[1] I do not know whether the above statement of the case carries the argument a step further than he does. I have some hope that a restatement of Kant's doctrine on these lines might go some way to meeting Broad's objections to it, and make unnecessary the introduction of moral intuitions to deal with the difficulties which Broad

[1] Broad, *FTET*, pp. 123–31.

finds. Kant would certainly have objected to my restatement, because it makes a moral decision depend on inclination; yet I do not myself find this objectionable; for I am not *defining* 'wrong' in terms of inclinations, but only saying what would in fact incline me to say that a certain act was wrong.

I do not, however, wish to defend this thesis here; I am not unaware of certain possible objections to it, objections to which, however, there are possible answers. I have introduced the thesis only as an illustration of the sort of bearing which an ethical theory, in the restricted sense of a theory concerning the analysis of moral terms, may have on moral decisions. In this example, ethics bears on morals in two ways. The first is by making the sort of suggestion which I have made in the two preceding paragraphs – a suggestion that the conditions which determine a person, given that he knows the facts of the case, to come to a certain moral decision can be divided into three classes, viz. understanding the meaning of words, imagination, and likes and dislikes. The second is by establishing, by the methods of logical analysis, that the words 'morally wrong' have such a meaning that the statement which I said was analytic is in fact analytic. Whether or not the piece of ethical theory which I have just put forward is tenable, the question 'Is it tenable?' has clearly a bearing on moral problems.

It is obvious that the discussion of the two ethical issues which I have just mentioned will bring a great deal of philosophy with it. The first one will involve us in a great variety of questions concerning the philosophy of mind: 'Does it make sense to speak of imagining oneself in another's position?', 'What is an inclination?', and so on. The second will lead us into the middle of a tangle of related logical questions – questions which are the lineal descendants of some of the most important problems of metaphysics – questions concerning the principle of individuation, the difference between things and qualities, and the identity of indiscernibles. Thus ethics is studied because it has a bearing on morals, and metaphysics and the philosophy of mind because they have a bearing on ethics – though in neither case are these the only reasons. Broad may therefore have been over-modest when he made so small a claim for the practical utility of ethical studies. At any rate, I should like to ask him whether he is now prepared to go a little further.

2   Philosophical Discoveries

I

There are two groups of philosophers in the world at present who often get across one another. I will call them respectively 'analysts' and 'metaphysicians', though this is strictly speaking inaccurate – for the analysts are in fact often studying the same old problems of metaphysics in their own way and with sharper tools, and the metaphysicians of an older style have no exclusive or proprietary right to the inheritance of Plato and Aristotle who started the business. Now metaphysicians often complain of analysts that, instead of doing *ontology*, studying *being qua being* (or for that matter *qua* anything else), they study only *words*. My purpose in this paper is to diagnose one (though only one) of the uneasinesses which lie at the back of this common complaint (a complaint which analysts of all kinds, and not only those of the 'ordinary-language' variety, have to answer). The source of the uneasiness seems to be this: there are some things in philosophy of which we want to say that we *know* that they are so – or even that we can *discover* or *come to know* that they are so – as contrasted with merely deciding arbitrarily that they are to be so; and yet we do not seem to know that these things are so by any observation of empirical fact. I refer to such things as that an object cannot both have and not have the same quality. These things used to be described as metaphysical truths; now it is more customary, at any rate among analysts, to express them metalinguistically, for example by saying that propositions of the form '*p* and not *p*' are analytically false. An analyst who

From *Mind*, LXIX, N.S., No. 274 (1960).

Sections II-V and VII of this paper appeared in the *Journal of Philosophy*, LIV (1957) 741, in a symposium with Professors Paul Henle and S. Körner entitled 'The Nature of Analysis'. The whole paper could not be printed there for reasons of space, and I am grateful to the editors of the *Journal* for permission to include in this revised version of the complete paper the extract already printed.

says this is bound to go on to say what he means by such expressions as 'analytically false'; and the account which he gives will usually be of the following general sort: to say that a proposition is analytically false is to say that it is false in virtue of the meaning or use which we give to the words used to express it, and of nothing else. But this way of speaking is not likely to mollify the metaphysician; indeed, he might be pardoned if he said that it made matters worse. For if philosophical statements are statements about how words are *actually* used by a certain set of people, then their truth will be contingent – whereas what philosophers seem to be after are necessary truths: but if they are expressions of a certain philosopher's *decision* to use words in a certain way, then it seems inappropriate to speak of our *knowing* that they are true. The first of these alternatives would seem to make the findings of philosophy contingent upon linguistic practices which might be other than they are; the second would seem to turn philosophy into the making of fiats or conventions about how a particular writer or group of writers is going to use terms – and this does not sound as if it would provide answers to the kind of questions that people used to be interested in, like 'Can an object both have and not have the same quality, and if not why not?' This is why to speak about 'decisions' (Henle, op. cit., pp. 753 ff.) or about 'rules' which are 'neither true nor false' (Körner, op. cit., pp. 760 ff.) will hardly assuage the metaphysician's legitimate anxiety, although both of these terms are likely to figure in any successful elucidation of the problem.

It is worth pointing out that this dilemma which faces the analyst derives, historically, from what used to be a principal tenet of the analytical movement in its early days – the view that all meaningful statements are either analytic (in the sense of analytically true or false) or else empirical. From this view it seems to follow that the statements of the philosopher must be either empirical or analytic; otherwise we can only call them meaningless, or else not really statements at all but some other kind of talk. Many analysts failed to see the difficulty to their position because of a confusion which it is easy to make. It is easy to suppose that the proposition that such and such another proposition is analytically true, or false (the proposition of the analyst), is itself analytic, and therefore fits readily into one of the approved categories of meaningful discourse. But, though it may *perhaps* be true, it is not *obviously* true that to say 'Propositions of the form "*p* and not *p*" are analytically false' is to make an analytically true statement; for is not this a statement about how the words 'and not' are used? And is it analytically true that they are used in this way? There are conflicting temptations to call the statement analytic, and empirical, and neither. The early analysts therefore ought to have felt more misgivings than most of them did feel about the status of their own activities; and this might have made them more sympathetic towards the metaphysicians, whose activities are of just the same dubious character (neither clearly empirical nor clearly analytic).

This is not to say that the matter has not been widely discussed since that time; and indeed there are certain well-known simple remedies for the perplexity. But I am not convinced that the disease is yet fully understood; and until it is, metaphysicians and analysts will remain at cross purposes. It is a pity that the early analysts, in general, tended to follow the lead, not of Wittgenstein, but of Carnap. Wittgenstein was moved by doubts on this point among others to describe his own propositions as 'nonsensical' (*Tractatus*, 6.54); but Carnap wrote, '[Wittgenstein] seems to me to be inconsistent in what he does. He tells us that one cannot state philosophical propositions and that whereof one cannot speak, thereof one must be silent; and then instead of keeping silent, he writes a whole philosophical book' (*Philosophy and Logical Syntax*, p. 37), thus indicating that he did not take Wittgenstein's misgivings as seriously as he should have. At any rate, the time has surely come when analysts and metaphysicians ought to co-operate in attacking this problem, which touches them both so nearly.

Once it is realised that the propositions of the analyst are not obviously analytic, a great many other possibilities suggest themselves. Are they, for example, empirical, as Professor Braithwaite has recently affirmed?[1] Or are some of them analytic and some empirical? Or are they sometimes ambiguous, so that the writer has no clear idea which of these two things (if either) they are? Or are they not statements at all, but resolves, stipulations or rules? Or, lastly, are they (to use an old label which has little if any explanatory force) synthetic *a priori*? These possibilities all require to be investigated.

[1] *An Empiricist's View of the Nature of Religious Belief* (Cambridge, 1955) p. 11. Reprinted in *The Existence of God*, ed. J. Hick, p. 236.

This paper is intended to serve only as a prolegomenon to such an investigation. It takes the form of an analogy. If we could find a type of situation in which the same sort of difficulty arises, but in a much clearer and simpler form, we might shed some light on the main problem. In choosing a much simpler model, we run the risk of over-simplification; but this is a risk which has to be taken if we are to make any progress at all. If we are careful to notice the differences, as well as the similarities, between the model and that of which it is a model, we shall be in less danger of misleading ourselves.

The suggestion which I am going tentatively to put forward might be described as a demythologised version of Plato's doctrine of *anamnesis*. Plato says that finding out the definition of a concept is like remembering or recalling. If this is correct, some of the difficulties of describing the process are accounted for. To remember (whether a fact, or how to do something) is not (or at any rate not obviously) to make an empirical discovery; yet it is not to make a decision either. So there may be here a way of escaping from the analyst's dilemma.

II

Suppose that we are sitting at dinner and discussing how a certain dance is danced. Let us suppose that the dance in question is one requiring the participation of a number of people – say one of the Scottish reels. And let us suppose that we have a dispute about what happens at a particular point in the dance; and that, in order to settle it, we decide to dance the dance after dinner and find out. We have to imagine that there is among us a sufficiency of people who know, or say they know, how to dance the dance – in the sense of 'know' in which one may know how to do something without being able to *say* how it is done.

When the dance reaches the disputed point everybody may dance as he thinks the dance should go; or they may all agree to dance according to the way that one party to the dispute says it should go. Whichever of these two courses they adopt, there are several things which may, in theory, happen. The first is, chaos – people bumping into one another so that it becomes impossible, as we should say, for the dance to proceed. The second is that there is no chaos, but a dance is danced which, though unchaotic, is not the dance which they were trying to dance – not, for example, the dance called 'the eightsome reel'. The third possibility is that the dance proceeds correctly. The difficulty is to say how we tell these three eventualities from one another, and whether the difference is empirical. It may be thought that, whether empirical or not, the difference is obvious; but I do not find it so.

It might be denied that there is any empirical difference between the first eventuality (chaos) and the second (wrong dance). For, it might be said, we could have a dance which consisted in people bumping into one another. In Michael Tippett's opera *The Midsummer Marriage* the character called the He-Ancient is asked reproachfully by a modern why his dancers never dance a new dance: in reply, he says he will show him a new dance, and immediately trips one of the dancers up, so that he falls on the ground and bruises himself. The implication of this manœuvre is the Platonic one that innovations always lead to chaos – that there is only one right way of dancing (the one that we have learnt from our elders and betters) and that all deviations from this are just wrong. But whether or not we accept this implication, the example perhaps shows that we *could* call *any* series of movements a dance. If, however, we started to call it a dance, we should have to stop calling it chaos. The terms 'dance' and 'chaos' mutually exclude one another; but although we cannot call any series of movements *both* chaos *and* dance, we can call any series of movements *either* chaos *or* dance; so the problem of distinguishing dance from chaos remains.

The first and the second eventualities (chaos and wrong dance) are alike in this, that, whether or not we can say that *any* series of movements is *a* dance, we cannot say that *any* series of movements is *the* dance (viz. the eightsome reel) about the correct way of dancing which we were arguing. It might therefore be claimed that, although it may be difficult to say what counts as *a* dance, and thus distinguish between the first and second eventualities, we can at least distinguish easily between either of them and the third (right dance). And so we can, *in theory*; for obviously both the wrong dance, and chaos or no dance at all, are distinct from the right dance. That is to say, the terms of my classification of things that might happen make

it analytic to say that these three things that might happen are
different things. But all distinctions are not empirical distinctions (for example, evaluative distinctions are not); and the
question is rather, 'How, empirically (if it is done empirically),
do we tell, of these three logically distinct happenings, which has
happened?' And how, in particular, do we tell whether the
third thing has happened (whether the dance has been danced
correctly)?

III

Let us first consider one thing that might be said. It might
be said: 'The dance has been danced correctly if what has been
danced is the dance *called* the eightsome reel.' On this suggestion,
all we have to know is how the expression 'eightsome reel' is
used; then we shall be able to recognise whether what has been
danced *is* an eightsome reel. This seems to me to be true; but
it will be obvious why I cannot rest content with this answer to
the problem. For I am using the dance analogy in an attempt
to elucidate the nature of the discovery called 'discovering the
use of words'; and therefore I obviously cannot, in solving the
problems raised within the analogy, appeal to our knowledge of
the use of the expression 'eightsome reel'. For this would not
be in the least illuminating; the trouble is that we do not know
whether knowing how the expression 'eightsome reel' is used is
knowing something empirical. We shall therefore have to go a
longer way round.

It may help if we ask, 'What does one have to assume if one
is to be sure that they have danced the right dance?' Let us
first introduce some restrictions into our analogy in order to
make the dance-situation more like the language-situation
which it is intended to illustrate. Let us suppose that the dance
is a traditional one which those of the company who can dance
it have all learnt in their early years; let us suppose that they
cannot remember the circumstances in which they learnt the
dance; nothing of their early dancing-lessons remains in their
memory except: how to dance the dance. And let us further
suppose that there are no books that we can consult to see if
they have correctly danced the dance – or, if there are books,
that they are not authoritative.

What, then, in such a situation, do we have to rely on in order to be sure that we have really established correctly what is the right way to dance the eightsome reel? Suppose that someone is detailed to put down precisely what happens in the dance that the dancers actually dance – what movements they make when. We then look at his description of the dance and, under certain conditions, say, 'Well then, *that* is how the eightsome reel is danced'. But what are these conditions?

We have to rely first of all upon the accuracy of the observer. We have to be sure that he has correctly put down what actually happened in the dance. And to put down correctly what one actually sees happening is, it must be admitted, empirical observation and description. But what else do we have to rely on? There are, it seems to me, at least two other requirements. As Henle correctly observes (I do not know why he thinks I would disagree), we cannot 'discover the rules of a ballroom dance simply by doing it' (op. cit., p. 753). The first requirement is that the dance which is being danced is indeed the eightsome reel; the second is that it is being danced right. These are not the same; for one may dance the eightsome reel but dance it wrong. Though the distinction between dancing a dance and dancing it right is not essential to my argument, it is in many contexts a crucial one (and with games, even more crucial than with dances; it must, e.g., be possible to play poker but, while playing it, cheat). Even Körner, who on p. 759 of his paper objects to the distinction, uses it himself on p. 762, where he says, 'If it [sc. a performance of a dance] is relevant but uncharacteristic, it is incorrect'. For both these requirements, we have to rely on the *memory* of the dancers; and, as I have said, to remember something is not (or at any rate not obviously) to make an empirical discovery.

IV

The sort of situation which I have been describing is different from the situation in which an anthropologist observes and describes the dances of a primitive tribe. This, it might be said, *is* an empirical enquiry. The anthropologist observes the behaviour of the members of the tribe, and *he* selects for study certain parts of this behaviour, namely those parts which, by reason of certain similarities, *he* classifies as dances. And within

c

the class of dances, *he* selects certain particular patterns of behaviour and names them by names of particular dances – names which *he* (it may be arbitrarily or for purely mnemonic reasons) chooses. Here we have nothing which is not included in the characteristic activities of the empirical scientist; we have the observation of similarities in the pattern of events, and the choosing of words to mark these similarities.

In the situation which I have been discussing, however, there are elements which there could not be in a purely anthropological enquiry. If a party of anthropologists sat down to dinner before starting their study of a particular dance, they could not fall into the sort of argument that I have imagined. Nor could they fall into it *after* starting the study of the dance. This sort of argument can arise only between people who, first of all, know how to dance the dance in question or to recognise a performance of it, but secondly are unable to say how it is danced. In the case of the anthropologists the first condition is not fulfilled. This difference between the two cases brings certain consequences with it. The anthropologists could not, as the people in my example do, know *what* dance it is that they are disputing about. In my example, the disputants know that what they are disputing about is how *the eightsome reel* is danced. They are able to say this, because they have learnt to dance a certain dance, and can still dance it, and know that if they dance it it will be distinctively different from a great many other dances which, perhaps, they can also dance. The anthropologists, on the other hand, have not learnt to dance the dance which they are going to see danced after dinner; and therefore, even if they have decided to *call* the dance that they are to see danced 'dance no. 23', this name is for them as yet unattached to any disposition of theirs to recognise the dance when it is danced. The anthropologists will not be able to say, when a particular point in the dance is reached, 'Yes, *that's* how it goes'. They will just put down what happens and add it to their records. But the people in my example, when they say 'eightsome reel', are not using an arbitrary symbol for *whatever* they are going to observe; the name 'eightsome reel' has for them already a determinate meaning, though they cannot as yet say what this meaning is. It is in this same way that a logician knows, before he sets out to investigate the logical properties of the concept of negation, *what* concept he is going to investigate.

The second consequence is that, when my dancers have put down in words the way a dance is danced, the words that they put down will have a peculiar character. It will not be a correct description of their remarks to say that they have just put down how a particular set of dancers danced on a particular occasion; for what has been put down is not: how a particular set of dancers *did* dance on a particular occasion, but: how *the* eightsome reel *is* danced. It is implied that if *any* dancers dance like *this* they are dancing an eightsome reel correctly. Thus what has been put down has the character of universality – one of the two positive marks of the *a priori* noted by Kant (we have already seen that what has been put down has the negative characteristic which Kant mentioned, that of not being empirical). What about the other positive mark? Is what we have put down (if we are the dancers) *necessarily* true? Is it necessarily true that the eightsome reel is danced in the way that we have put down?

What we have put down is 'The eightsome reel is danced in the following manner, viz. . . .' followed by a complete description of the steps and successive positions of the dancers. We may feel inclined to say that this statement is necessarily true. For, when we have danced the dance, and recognised it as an eightsome reel correctly danced, we may feel inclined to say that, if it had been danced differently, we *could* not have called it, correctly, an eightsome reel (or at any rate not a correct performance of one); and that, on the other hand, danced as it was, we could not have denied that it was an eightsome reel. The statement which we have put down seems as necessary as the statement 'A square is a rectangle with equal sides'. I do not wish my meaning to be mistaken at this point. I am not maintaining that there is any temptation to say that the statement 'The dance which we have just danced is an eightsome reel' is a necessary statement; for there is no more reason to call this necessary than there is in the case of any other singular statement of fact. The statement which I am saying is necessary is 'The eightsome reel is danced as follows, viz. . . .' followed by a complete description.

We may, then, feel inclined to say that this statement, since it has all the qualifications, is an *a priori* statement. But there is also a temptation to say that it is synthetic. For consider again for a moment the situation as it was before we began to dance.

Then we already knew how to dance the eightsome reel, and so for us the term 'eightsome reel' had already a determinate meaning; and it would be plausible to say that, since we knew the meaning of 'eightsome reel' already before we started dancing, anything that we subsequently discovered could not be something attributable to the meaning of the term 'eightsome reel'; and therefore that it could not be something analytic; and therefore that it must be something synthetic. Have we not, after all, *discovered* something about how the eightsome reel is danced?

There is thus a very strong temptation to say that the statement 'The eightsome reel is danced in the following way, viz. . . .' followed by a complete description, is, when made by people in the situation which I have described, a synthetic *a priori* statement. Perhaps this temptation ought to be resisted, for it bears a very strong resemblance to the reasons which made Kant say that 'Seven plus five equals twelve' is a synthetic *a priori* statement. Yet the existence of the temptation should be noted. Certainly to call this statement 'synthetic *a priori*' would be odd; for similar grounds could be given for considering all statements about how words are used as synthetic *a priori* statements. If, which I have seen no reason to believe, there is a class of synthetic *a priori* statements, it can hardly be as large as this. Probably what has to be done with the term 'synthetic *a priori*' is to recognise that it has been used to cover a good many different kinds of statement, and that the reasons for applying it to them differ in the different cases. It is, in fact, an ambiguous label which does not even accurately distinguish a class of statements, let alone explain their character. What would explain this would be to understand the natures of the situations (as I said, not all of the same kind) in which we feel inclined to use the term; and this is what I am now trying, in one particular case, to do.

v

The peculiar characteristics of the situation which I have been discussing, like the analogous characteristics of the language-situation which I am trying to illuminate, all arise from the fact (on which Professor Ryle has laid so much stress) that we can know something (e.g. how to dance the eightsome reel or use a word) without being able yet to say what we know. Professor Henle has objected to the extension of Ryle's distinction to the language-situation. 'This distinction is no longer clear', he says, 'when one comes to language, and it is by no means apparent that one can always know how to use a word without being able to say how it is used' (op. cit., p. 750). But although I do not claim that the distinction is entirely clear in any field, in language it is perhaps clearer than elsewhere. To say how a term is used we have, normally, to *mention* the term inside quotation marks, and to *use*, in speaking of the quoted sentence or statement in which it occurs, some such logician's term as 'means the same as' or 'is analytic'. In saying how a term is used, we do not have to use it; and conversely we may know fully how to use it in all contexts without being able to say how it is used. For example, a child may have learnt the use of 'father', and use it correctly, but not be able to say how it is used because he has not learnt the use of 'mean' or any equivalent expression. Henle seems to confuse being able to 'decide on logical grounds' that a statement is true with being able to say 'the statement is logically true'. A person who did not know the use of the expression 'logically true' could do the former but not the latter.

Besides noticing that the dance-situation has the characteristics which I have described, we should also be alive to certain dangers. There is first the danger of thinking that it could not have been the case that the eightsome reel was danced in some quite different way. It is, of course, a contingent fact, arising out of historical causes with which I at any rate am unacquainted, that the dance called 'the eightsome reel' has the form it has and not some other form. If it had some different form, what my dancers would have learnt in their childhood would have been different, and what they would have learnt to call 'the eightsome reel' would have been different too; yet the statement 'the eightsome reel is danced in the following manner, etc.' would have had just the same characteristics as I have mentioned (though the 'etc.' would stand for some different description of steps and movements).

Next, there is the danger of thinking that if *anthropologists* were observing the dance, and had been told that the dance which they were to observe was called 'the eightsome reel', *they*, in reporting their observations, would be making the same kind of statement – namely a non-empirical, universally necessary statement which at the same time we are tempted to call synthetic. They would not be making this sort of statement at all, but an ordinary empirical statement to the effect that the Scots have a dance which they dance in a certain manner and call 'the eightsome reel'.

VI

There is also a third thing which we must notice. If a completely explicit definition were once given of the term 'eightsome reel', it would have to consist of a specification of what constitutes a correct performance of this dance. To give such a definition is to give what is often called a 'rule' for the performance of the dance. Now if we already have such a definition, then statements like 'The eightsome reel is danced in the following way, viz. . . .', followed by a specification of the steps, will be seen to be analytic, provided only that we understand 'is danced' in the sense of 'is correctly danced'. It might therefore be said that, once the definition is given, there remains no problem – no proposition whose status defies classification. Similarly, if we were to *invent* a dance and give it explicit rules of performance, there would be no problem. But in this latter case there would be no *discovery* either. It is because, in my problem-case, we do not *start off* by having a definition, yet do start off by having a determinate meaning for the term 'eightsome reel', that the puzzle arises. It is in the *passage to* the definition that the mystery creeps in – in the passage (to use Aristotle's terms) from the ἡμῖν γνώριμον to the ἁπλῶς γνώριμον.[1] What we have to start with is not a definition, but the mere ability to recognise instances of correct performances of the dance; what we have at the end is the codification in a definition of what we know. So what we have at the end is different from what we have at the beginning, and it sounds sensible to speak of our *discovering* the definition – just as those who first defined the circle as the locus of a point equidistant, etc., thought that they had discovered something about the circle, namely what later came to be called its essence. We see here how definitions came to be treated as synthetic statements; and, since the real or essential definition (the prototype of all synthetic *a priori* statements) is one of the

[1] i.e. from knowledge such as we have to knowledge in an unqualified sense (*Eth. Nic.* 1095 b2; *An. Post.* 71 b33).

most characteristic constituents of metaphysical thinking, this explains a great deal about the origins of metaphysics.

Briefly, there are two statements whose status is unproblematical, both expressed in the same words. There is first the anthropologist's statement that the eightsome reel (meaning 'a certain dance to which the Scots give that name') is (as a matter of observed fact) danced in a certain manner. This is a plain empirical statement. Secondly, there is the statement such as might be found in a book of dancing instructions – the statement that the eightsome reel is danced (meaning 'is correctly danced') in a certain manner. This statement is analytic, since by 'eightsome reel' the writer *means* 'the dance which is (correctly) danced in the manner described'. Should we then say that the appearance of there being a third, mysterious, metaphysical, synthetic *a priori* statement about the dance, somehow intermediate between these two, is the result merely of a confusion between them, a confusion arising easily from the fact that they are expressed in the same words ? This, it seems to me, would be a mistake. For how do we *get* to the second, analytic statement ? Only via the definition or rule; but if the definition is not a mere empirical description, then there is, on this view, nothing left for it to be but a stipulative definition, the result of a decision. So there will be again no such thing as discovering how the eightsome reel is danced. There will only be something which might be described as 'inventing the eightsome reel'. It is preferable, therefore, to say that there is a third kind of statement, intermediate between the first and the second, which forms, as it were, the transition to the second – we settle down in the comfortable analyticity of the second only after we have discovered that this definition of the term 'eightsome reel', and no other, is the one that accords with our pre-existing but unformulated idea of how the dance should be danced. And this discovery seems to be neither a mere decision, nor a mere piece of observation. But since I am still very perplexed by this problem, I do not rule out the possibility that, were I to become clearer about it, I should see that there is no third alternative.

Before I conclude this section of my paper, and go on to describe more complicated kinds of dances which resemble talking even more closely, I have two remarks to make. The first is that, unless *some* people knew how to dance dances, anthropologists could not observe empirically how dances are

danced; and that therefore there could not be empirical statements about dances unless there were at least the possibility of
the kind of non-empirical statement that I have been charac-
terising. The situation is like that with regard to moral judgements; unless *some* people make genuine evaluative moral
judgements, there is no possibility of other people making what
have been called 'inverted commas' moral judgements, i.e.
explicit or implicit descriptions of the moral judgements that
the first set of people make.[1] So, if philosophical analysis
resembles the description of dances in the respects to which I
have drawn attention, empirical statements about the use of
words cannot be made unless there is at least the possibility of
these other, non-empirical statements about the use of words.
This perhaps explains the odd fact that analytical enquiries
seem often to start by collecting empirical data about word-
uses, but to end with apparently *a priori* conclusions.

The second remark is that I have nothing to say in this paper
which sheds any direct light on the question (often confused with
the one which I am discussing) – the question of the distinction
between logic and philology. The features which I am trying
to pick out are features as well of philological as of logical discoveries, and this makes them more, not less, perplexing.

VII

I will now draw attention to some differences between the
comparatively simple dance-situation which I have been discussing so far and the language-situation which is the subject of
this paper. Talking is an infinitely more complex activity than
dancing. It is as if there were innumerable different kinds of
steps in dancing, and a dancer could choose at any moment (as
is to a limited extent the case in ballroom dancing) to make any
one of these steps. Talking is in this respect more like ballroom
dancing than like reels – there is a variety of different things one
can do, and if one's partner knows how to dance, she reacts
appropriately; but to do *some* things results in treading on one's
partner's toes, or bumping into other couples and such further
obstacles as there may be, however, well she knows how to
dance. Nevertheless there are a great many things which one

[1] See my *Language of Morals*, p. 124 f.

can do; and not all of them are laid down as permissible in rules which have been accepted before we do them. There can be innovations in dancing and in speech – and some of the innovations are understood even though they are innovations.

Both dancing and talking can become forms of creative art. There are kinds of dancing and of talking in which the performer is bound by no rules except those which he cares to make up as he goes along. Some poetry is like this; and so is 'creative tap-dancing' (the title of a book which once came into my hands). The most creative artists, however, are constrained to talk or dance *solo*. It is not about these highest flights of talking and dancing that I wish to speak, but about those more humdrum activities which require the co-operation of more than one person, and in which, therefore, the other people involved have to know a good deal about what sort of thing to expect one to do, and what they are expected to do in answer. It is in this sense that I am speaking of 'knowing how to dance' and 'knowing how to talk'.

What makes co-operation possible in both these activities is that the speaker or dancer should not do things which make the other people say 'We don't know what to make of this'. That is to say, he must not do things which cannot be easily related to the unformulated rules of speaking or dancing which everybody knows who has learnt to perform these activities. The fact that these rules are unformulated means that to learn to formulate them is to make some sort of discovery – a discovery which, as I have said, cannot be described without qualification as an empirical one. If a person in speaking or dancing does something of which we say 'We don't know what to make of this', there are only two ways of re-establishing that *rapport* between us which makes these co-operative activities possible: either he must explain to us what we *are* to make of what he has done; or else he must stop doing it and do something more orthodox. He must either teach us his new way of dancing or talking, or go on dancing or talking in our old way. I should like to emphasise that I am not against what Körner calls 'replacement-analysis'; the last chapter of my *Language of Morals* is evidence of this. But we need to be very sure that we understand the functioning of the term that is being replaced before we claim that a new gadget will do the old job better.

It might be said, dancing is not like talking, because dancing is a gratuitous activity, and talking a purposeful one; therefore there are things which can go wrong in talking that cannot go wrong in dancing – things which prevent the purposes of talking being realised. This I do not wish to deny; though the existence of this difference does not mean that there are not also the similarities to which I have been drawing attention. And the difference is in any case not absolute. Some talking is gratuitous; and some dancing is purposeful. When dancing in a crowded ballroom, we have at least the purpose of avoiding obstacles, human and inanimate. If we imagine these obstacles multiplied, so that our dance-floor becomes more like its analogue, that elusive entity which we call 'the world', dancing becomes very like talking. And all dance-floors have at least a floor and boundaries of some kind; so no kind of dancing is *completely* gratuitous; all dancers have the purpose of not impinging painfully against whatever it is limits their dance-floor (unless there are penitential dances which consist in bruising oneself against the walls – but this, too, would be a purpose). And there are some markedly purposeful activities which, though not called dances, are like dances in the features to which I have drawn attention – for example, the pulling up of anchors (old style).

This analogy points to a way of thinking about our use of language which is a valuable corrective to the more orthodox representational view, in which 'facts', 'qualities', and other dubious entities fit like untrustworthy diplomats between language and the world. We do not need these intermediaries; there are just people in given situations trying to understand one another. Logic, in one of the many senses of that word, is learning to formulate the rules that enable us to make something of what people say. Its method is to identify and describe the various sorts of things that people say (the various dances and their steps) such as predication, conjunction, disjunction, negation, counting, adding, promising, commanding, commending – need I ever stop ? In doing this it has to rely on our knowledge, as yet unformulated, of how to do these things – things of which we may not even know the names, and which indeed may not *have* names till the logician invents them; but which are, nevertheless, distinct and waiting to be given names. Since this knowledge is knowledge of something that we have learnt, it has, as I have said, many of the characteristics of memory – though it would be incorrect, strictly speaking, to say that we *remember* how to use a certain word; Plato's term 'recall (ἀναμιμνήσκε-σθαι)' is, perhaps, more apt. As in the case of memory, however, we know, without being, in many cases, able to give further evidence, that we have got it right. And often the only test we can perform is: trying it out again. In most cases there comes a point at which we are satisfied that we have got the thing right (in the case of speaking, that we have formulated correctly what we know). Of course, the fact that we are satisfied does not show that we are not wrong; but if once satisfied, we remain satisfied until we discover, or are shown, some cause for dissatisfaction.

VIII

Meno, in the Platonic dialogue named after him, is asked by Socrates what goodness is (a question much more closely akin than is commonly allowed to the question, 'How and for what purposes is the word "good" used ?'). Being a young man of a sophistical turn of mind, Meno says: 'But Socrates, how are you going to look for something, when you don't in the least know what it is ? . . . Or even if you do hit upon it, how are you going to know that this is *it*, without having previous knowledge of what *it* is ?'[1] In more modern terms, if we do not already know the use of the word 'good' (or, in slightly less fashionable language, its analysis), how, when some account of its use (some analysis) is suggested, shall we know whether it is the correct account ? Yet (as Socrates goes on to point out) if we knew already, we should not have asked the question in the first place. So philosophy either cannot begin, or cannot reach a conclusion.

It will be noticed that my dancers could be put in the same paradoxical position. If they know already how the dance is danced, what can they be arguing about ? But if they do not know already, how will they know, when they have danced the dance, whether they have danced it correctly ? The solution to the paradox lies in distinguishing between knowing how to dance a dance and being able to say how it is danced. Before the enquiry begins, they are able to do the former, but not the latter; after the enquiry is over they can do the latter, and they know that they are right because all along they could do the

[1] *Meno*, 80 d.

former. And it is the same with the analysis of concepts. We
know how to use a certain expression, but are unable to say how
it is used (λογὸν δίδοναι, give an analysis or definition, formulate in words the use of the expression). Then we try to do the
latter; and we know we have succeeded when we have found
an analysis which is in accordance with our hitherto unformulated knowledge of how to use the word. And finding out whether
the account of the dance is right involves dancing.

Dialectic, like dancing, is typically a co-operative activity.
It consists in trying out the proposed account of the use of a
word by using the word in accordance with it, and seeing what
happens. It is an experiment with words, though not, as we
have seen, an altogether empirical experiment. In the same way,
we might dance the dance according to someone's account of
how it is danced, and see if we can say afterwards whether what
we have danced is the dance that we were arguing about (e.g.
the eightsome reel) or at least *a* dance, or whether it is no dance
at all. There is no space here to give many examples of dialectic;
but I will give the most famous one of all.[1] It is a destructive
use of the technique, resulting in the *rejection* of a suggested
analysis. An account of the use of the word 'right' is being tried
out which says that 'right' means the same as 'consisting in
speaking the truth and giving back anything that one has
received from anyone'. The analysis is tried out by 'dancing'
a certain statement, viz. 'It is always right to give a madman
back his weapons which he entrusted to us when sane'. But
the dance has clearly gone wrong; for this statement is certainly
not (as the proposed definition would make it) analytic, since to
deny it, as most people would, is not to contradict oneself. So
the analysis has to be rejected.

Plato was right in implying that in recognising that such a
proposition is not analytic we are relying on our memories. It
is an example of the perceptive genius of that great logician, that
in spite of being altogether at sea concerning the *source* of our
philosophical knowledge; and in spite of the fact that his use of
the material mode of speech misled him as to the *status* of the
analyses he was looking for – that in spite of all this he spotted
the very close logical analogies between philosophical discoveries
and remembering. He was wrong in supposing that we are
remembering something that we learnt in a former life – just as

[1] Adapted from *Republic*, 331 c.

more recent mythologists have been wrong in thinking that we
are discerning the structure of some entities called 'facts'. What
we are actually remembering is what we learnt on our mothers'
knees, and cannot remember learning.

Provisionally, then, we might agree with the metaphysicians
that philosophy has to contain statements which are neither
empirical statements about the way words are actually used, nor
yet expressions of decisions about how they are to be used; but
we should refuse to infer from this that these statements are
about some non-empirical order of being. The philosopher
elucidates (not by mere observation) the nature of something
which exists before the elucidation begins (for example, there is
such an operation as negation before the philosopher investi-
gates it; the philosopher no more invents negation than
Aristotle made man rational). He neither creates the objects of
his enquiry, nor receives them as mere data of experience; yet
for all that, to say that there is such an operation as negation is
no more mysterious than to say that there is such a dance as the
eightsome reel. But even that is quite mysterious enough.

3　A School for Philosophers

Once, while lecturing in Germany some years ago, I was told, by an Englishman who was in a position to know, that in the opinion of most German philosophers philosophy was not studied in England at all. I think this was an exaggeration; but it is certainly true that the subject as studied in England has such a different aspect from what is studied in Germany under the same name, that one might be forgiven for thinking that they are really two quite different subjects. I shall give reasons later on for arguing that this appearance is deceptive; that it is really the same subject studied in two different ways: but the main object of this paper is to describe the conditions under which people learn and study philosophy in Britain, taking Oxford as an illustration.[1] For I think that, given the educational system (we might almost say 'given the administrative arrangements') of the older British universities, it would be wellnigh impossible for philosophy as it is known in Germany to flourish there with any vigour.

My wife has a cousin who studied philosophy under Husserl at Freiburg. I have heard him say that, when he first went to see the great man, Husserl produced about six bound volumes and said: 'Here are my books; come back in a year's time.' He went there, of course, as a graduate student; I do not know whether his experience was typical, or whether in German universities an undergraduate would get as little attention from his teachers as this: but at any rate nothing could be more different from the treatment accorded to the ordinary student starting philosophy at Oxford. We have at Oxford about sixty professional philo-

From *Ratio*, ii, No. 2 (1960). This article is a revised version of a lecture given at a number of German centres in the summer of 1957, under the title 'The Study of Philosophy in Great Britain'.

[1] For further remarks on this subject, see my review in *Philosophische Rundschau*, v (1957) 269, of two recent surveys of analytical philosophy. The review is in German.

sophers; the bulk of these, apart from the three professors at the top, and a very few university readers, lecturers, etc., are, like myself, fellows and tutors in one or other of the many colleges which make up the university. Each of us has committed to his charge some twenty or so students from his own college; these are normally studying some other subject in addition to philosophy – for we do not think it healthy to study philosophy in complete isolation; we put it with some other, less abstract subject such as history or economics or psychology. It should, perhaps, be mentioned also that philosophy is studied at Oxford by very large numbers of students. It is not, as at most other places, a small specialist course. Most of my pupils are going to be, not professional philosophers, but businessmen, politicians, schoolmasters, clergymen, lawyers, journalists, civil servants, and, indeed, almost anything but philosophers; and a substantial number of these may be expected to reach the highest ranks of their professions. So the Oxford tutor, if he can teach his pupils how to think more clearly and to the point, can have much more influence on the life of the country in this way than he is likely to achieve by writing books, unless the books are outstandingly successful.

Each of these students goes to his philosophy tutor once a week, either by himself or in the company of one other student, for what is known as a *tutorial*. He will have been told the week before to read certain books or articles and to write an essay on some subject chosen by the tutor to bring out the most important questions raised in the books. At the beginning of the tutorial he will read this essay aloud; this will take about fifteen minutes. If he gets to the end of it without interruption, the rest of the hour will be spent in discussing the subject of the essay. The average tutor's working week during term will consist of from ten to twenty hours spent seeing pupils in this way, and about two hours' public lectures or seminars. The rest of his time, after some part of it has been devoted to practical business in connection with the administration of the college, is his own.

Although we have a far smaller number of professional administrators than most other universities, and although we keep in closer touch with our undergraduates, both administratively and personally, than is common elsewhere, this does not mean that the academic staff are burdened to a higher degree

with administrative duties. The situation is rather that, by
having the university divided into a large number of colleges
of some 200 to 400 students each, and by handling nearly all
administrative problems at this elementary level, we prevent
our administrative machinery growing to such a portentous size
that it requires the services of great numbers of professionals to
manage it. For example, for some years I myself looked after
the repair and maintenance of my own college buildings. This
took no more of my time than I was quite willing to spend on it
as a hobby; and besides, it is good for a philosopher to be made
to perform feats of mountaineering while inspecting the state
of the roofs, and thus to realise that if somebody does not prevent
the rain from getting in, the college will eventually disintegrate.
In a similar spirit, two of my best-known philosophical colleagues, Mr Strawson and Mr (now Professor) Nowell-Smith,
for long periods managed, respectively, the domestic arrangements and the estates and investments of their colleges. All these
jobs would be done by professionals at most other universities,
because of their centralised administration; but on the whole we
prefer it our way, and the jobs are as well done. Certainly I have
met the complaint more often elsewhere than at Oxford that 'we
spend so much time on administration that we can't do any
philosophy'.

Out of term – that is to say for about twenty-eight weeks in
the year – we are free to philosophise, or to do anything else
that takes our fancy; for our jobs are secure and cannot be
taken from us until we reach the age of sixty-seven, unless we
are guilty of some outrageous personal misconduct. We are
under no pressure – beyond that of ambition – to write books
or articles. In some other places the staff are in danger of
spoiling their chances of promotion, or even further employment, unless they keep up a constant output of published
writing; and this naturally inflates the publishers' catalogues.
I will not say that in Oxford no philosopher ever writes anything unless he has something to say; but at any rate he cannot
claim that he has to do it to earn a living. We regard teaching,
not writing, as our main job – what we are paid for.

What, then, is the effect of this system on the student and on
his tutor? It is profound. The student is very soon made to
realise that everything that he says in an essay has to be justified
before a highly skilled and usually merciless critic, not only in

respect of its truth, but also in respect of relevance, accuracy, significance and clarity. Anything that is put in to fill in space, or which is ambiguous or vague or pretentious, or which contains more sound than significance, or whose object is anything else but to express genuine thought, is ruthlessly exposed for what it is. The tutor knows that he cannot be sure of getting his pupil to see the truth; for, even if it were not possible in philosophy for there to be sincere differences of opinion about the truth, nobody can see the truth about a philosophical question until he has by his own efforts reached the point from which it is visible. What the tutor can do is to teach his pupil to think effectively; to express his thought clearly to himself and to others; to make distinctions where there are distinctions to be made, and thus avoid unnecessary confusion – and not to use long words (or short ones) without being able to explain what they mean. Enormous stress is laid on style, not in the sense of literary elegance – for this is esteemed of small value – but in the sense of an effective, unambiguous, clear and ordered expression of one's thought, which cannot be achieved unless the thought itself has the same qualities.

The effect of this treatment on the student is what might be expected. But its effect on the tutor himself should not escape notice. He has continually to set an example of the virtues which he is seeking to inculcate. Though he may have been studying a question for twenty years or more, he has hour after hour – sometimes for five hours or even seven in a day – to explain it afresh to a succession of people who are considering it for the first time. For a historian or a language-scholar such a routine might well be called deadening – though for a man whose vocation it is to teach, the task has a continuing and absorbing interest. But for a philosopher this life is just what is required to perfect his understanding of the subject. I can honestly say that I have learnt more from my pupils than I have from books. For is it not true that the really fundamental steps in any philosophical theory are those taken at the outset? It is the *ways in* to philosophy that are the most interesting part of the subject; for it is the course taken at the outset – in the first steps from ordinary ways of speaking to the extraordinary things which philosophers habitually say – that determines the whole of a thinker's theories. For example, how do we find ourselves saying 'Free will is an illusion' or 'Time is unreal' or any other of the things that philosophers say in their books ? Under the Oxford system, the professional philosopher is compelled continually to explore these foundations of the subject, to see if they are sound. Not for him the delights of erecting, in solitary thought, imposing edifices – of writing huge volumes which only a handful of people will ever understand. He has to spend his time asking the question 'How can philosophy begin ?'; for he has to spend it getting people to philosophise who have probably never done it before.

It will be seen how inimical our method of teaching is to the turning of philosophy into a *mystique*. If a philosopher finds that some philosophical theory cannot be explained to the ordinary person, as represented by his beginner-pupils, that does not necessarily show that there is anything wrong with the theory; but if he knows that it has got to be explained, his efforts to find a foolproof way of explaining it *may* lead him to reconsider the theory itself, or at any rate to improve its formulation. At the same time, he cannot afford to be too superficial in the interests of simplification; for he has to teach his pupils to *think*, not just to repeat a few catch-phrases; he knows that at the end of three years they will be examined, not by himself, but by two or three of his colleagues who may have quite different opinions from his own; and that the only thing that will count in the candidate's favour is real thought, expressed in a clear and orderly manner. Moreover, to have one's pupils repeat catch-phrases to one, day after day (especially one's own catch-phrases), would be boring to an unendurable degree – the one thing we all most hate is for our pupils to find out what our own views are and parrot them in their essays. It makes the views sound so silly.

If a pupil survives this ordeal, and wants to become a professional himself, he will settle down to another two years or so devoted entirely to philosophy (though if he is of outstanding ability, he may be offered a job without this preliminary). He will spend his time, not in composing a long thesis or dissertation on some part of the subject, but in finding his way about the subject as a whole. The short thesis that he does is intended only to satisfy the examiners that he can do, and express, a bit of thinking longer than is required for answering examination questions. The theses of successful candidates are often subsequently published in the form of one or two articles in periodicals. The degree for which he is studying, however, and which he hopes will help him in securing employment, is given in the main on the results of a severe written and oral examination. For this examination the man prepares by wide reading and, above all, by talking. He will go most days to seminars and discussions, and will spend as much time as he can arguing on philosophical questions with his contemporaries and with anybody else he can get hold of. When I say *talking* and *arguing*, I mean a co-operative activity. The budding philosopher whose idea of argument is to deliver long monologues, and who does not know how to listen to, and answer, the questions and objections that are put to him (διδόναι καὶ δέχεσθαι λόγον), will find that his company is avoided. Nobody in Oxford can collect a private coterie to listen to him – not even the most distinguished professors. Even quite humble students go to the seminars of professors to attack and dispute, and not to imbibe a doctrine; and this is how the professors themselves like to be treated. And one will often find at one's seminars, not only students, but a number of one's colleagues ready to do battle; if one wishes to find out what are the principal objections to a view which one has temporarily espoused, the quickest way to find out is to give a seminar on the subject – one will discover enough to keep one busy.

When I have read a paper or given a lecture to a German audience, what has frequently happened after the paper has been something like this: each of the audience who wants to say something has made a little speech, lasting some minutes, setting out his point of view on the subject of the paper, or about philosophy in general. After everyone who wants to has had his say, the proceedings have closed with a formal reply by the speaker. There has seldom, in my experience, been any dialogue or argument – just a succession of different views, none of which, not even the principal speaker's, is subjected to any elenchus. In Oxford it is very different. After a paper has been read, somebody may reply briefly to the paper, or the meeting may be immediately thrown open to discussion. What happens thereafter is rather like what happens in the Socratic dialogues of Plato – or perhaps, since Plato has organised his dialogues in a rather literary way, like the original Socratic discussions on which the dialogues are modelled. Speeches of more than a few sentences are rare; if anybody says more than about five sentences in succession, people begin to look embarrassed. We have instead a series of dialogues of the question-and-answer type, usually between two people, but sometimes with more intervening; and when one of the participants has nothing further to say, or begins to flag, or cannot answer his opponent, the cudgels are taken up by somebody else. When the thing is done properly, which it is not always, there is a great feeling for relevance. To introduce a new topic which does not grow naturally out of the one being discussed (unless that is obviously exhausted) is to risk being politely ignored. And one is not supposed to butt into a dialogue which is already, so to speak, fully manned. The rules of this game are so well understood, among the professionals at any rate, that the office of chairman is purely titular; the chairman joins in the discussion on the same terms as everyone else if he feels like it; otherwise he has nothing to do. The size of the meeting, which may be up to fifty people, does not make much difference to this, since at any one time only a handful of people are actively concerned in the discussion; the rest listen.

Here again, as in all our philosophy, the virtues which we seek are clarity, relevance and brevity – and, of course, at this level, some degree of originality; for these discussions take up so large a part of our time that the obvious moves in the various philosophical chess games that are in fashion are well known, and can be taken for granted. I say 'games', not because I think philosophy is not a serious matter, but because philosophical arguments, conducted in the way that I have described, have the same sort of objectivity that chess games have. If you are beaten at chess you are beaten, and it is not to be concealed by any show of words; and in a philosophical discussion of this sort, provided that an unambiguously stated thesis is put forward, objective refutation is possible. Indeed, the whole object of our philosophical training is to teach us to put our theses in a form in which they can be submitted to this test. Ambiguities and evasions and rhetoric, however uplifting, are regarded as the mark of a philosopher who has not learnt his craft; we prefer professional competence to a superficial brilliance.

The conditions I have described are those obtaining in Oxford. At other universities you will find differences, some of them considerable. But the tone of British philosophy is at

present set by Oxford (thirty years ago it was Cambridge); and
the sort of philosophy that is done in England now is the result,
more than anything else, of the kind of philosophical training
which I have been picturing. British philosophers, by and large,
will not be bothered with a philosophical thesis which is not
stated briefly and in clear terms, such as make it possible to
discuss it in the manner I have described; and it is much more
highly esteemed if it is the sort of thesis which can be explained
without technicalities, if possible in everyday language. We
have not taken to mathematical logic with any enthusiasm,
though a number of us can do it. The reason for this bias towards
everyday language is that our dealings with our pupils have
shown us that it is in the passage from everyday language to
technical language that all the most vexatious problems of philosophy have their origin. Thus, when we examine a work of
mathematical logic, we shall normally take it for granted that
the writer has made no errors in the calculations; what we shall
observe closely is the process by which he sets up his calculus,
often using terms of common speech to do so. And the same
may be said of our attitude to any other kind of technical
vocabulary.

So on the whole we do not write long or difficult books; if our
ideas are understood by our colleagues in the course of verbal
discussion, that is enough for us. We write books and articles
only to *fix* a thesis so that people will know exactly what they
are discussing. You need a book from time to time to hang the
discussion on; and when anybody thinks he has got to a point
in the discussion when a good statement of a position in which
he believes can be written, he writes something. But even in
writing it, we know that, however pedantically we might seek
to answer all the objections that our colleagues will inevitably
think up against our views, we should never succeed; so on the
whole we share Plato's attitude towards the written word; it is
a *pis aller*, and the best thing to do is to be as brief and clear as
possible and answer the objections verbally as they arise in the
course of the inevitable discussion. In this way, objections will
often reach the author in the course of a few months which do
not appear in the periodicals for many years, if ever.

For all our dislike of writing, we in fact contrive to write as
much as most other philosophers. But our attitude to our writings, and to those of other people, is different. We do not think

it a *duty* to write books; still less do we think it a duty to read more than a few of the books which others write – for we know that, given our heavy load of teaching, to read more than the essential books would take us away from more important things. Our duty is to discuss philosophy with our colleagues and to teach our pupils to do the same – books and articles are an unconsidered by-product of this process; their content is generally quite familiar from verbal discussion years before they get published. We find out which 'the essential books' are by each reading a very few and telling the others about them.

The result is that, if one wants a book to be read by one's colleagues, it will have to be short, clear and to the point. They will especially like it if, besides reading it themselves, they can give it to their undergraduate students to read; so the more practical and down-to-earth it is the better. The best way to get one's ideas discussed in Oxford (and this is the limit of the ambition of most of us) is to write a book which every student of philosophy in the university will have to read; this means that every person teaching philosophy in the place will have to discuss it several times a week with his pupils, and will have to work out, until he is quite familiar with them, all the arguments that can be brought for, or against, the main points in it. If one can write this sort of book, it will be discussed, not only by the students, but by one's colleagues, who are the ablest collection of philosophers in the country; and that is fame. The certain way to obscurity, on the other hand, is to write long obscure books. Nobody will ever read them.

One of my purposes in saying all this is to give my own explanation of what usually happens on those occasions (unfortunately rare) when a typical Oxford philosopher meets a typical German philosopher in a philosophical discussion. The German philosopher will say something relating to his own philosophical views; the British philosopher will then say that he cannot understand what has been said, and will ask for an elucidation. The German will take this, the first time that it happens to him, for an encouragement, and will go on expounding his views; but he will be disappointed by the reaction. What was desired, it turns out, was not more of the same sort of thing; what the British philosopher wanted was to take just one sentence that the German had uttered – say the first sentence – or perhaps, for a start, just one word in this sentence; and he wanted an explanation given of the way in which this word was being used. One of the sources of this procedure is to be found in a piece of advice given by Wittgenstein:

> The right method of philosophy would be this. To say nothing except what can be said . . . i.e. something that has nothing to do with philosophy: and then always, when someone else wished to say something metaphysical, to demonstrate to him that he had given no meaning to certain signs in his propositions. (*Tractatus*, 6.53)

Present-day Oxford philosophers do not now take such a destructive view as this; they are perfectly prepared to have metaphysical things said; in fact, as I shall argue, what we spend most of our time in Oxford doing is metaphysics. But we have absorbed Wittgenstein's advice to this extent, that we have the greatest aversion to cutting ourselves off from our base in ordinary speech; we have seen what monstrous philosophical edifices have been erected by slipping, surreptitiously, from the ordinary uses of words to extraordinary uses which are never explained; we spend most of our working time explaining our *own* uses of words to our pupils; and when we find ourselves in the position of pupil, nothing pleases us so much as to sit back and have a German metaphysician explain to us, if he can, how he is going to get his metaphysical system started. And as he is usually unable to do this, the discussion never gets on to what he thinks of as the meat of the theory. This is a great disappointment to him, and leads easily to the accusation that we in Oxford are antagonistic to metaphysics. But actually we do a lot of metaphysics ourselves, only we have an obsession that it must be done rigorously as we understand the word; this means, among other things, that nothing should be said whose meaning cannot be explained. I wish to emphasise that, although we do as a matter of fact in Oxford do metaphysics in plainer language than is fashionable in other places, we by no means insist on people saying nothing that cannot be said in plain language; there is no ban on using words in any way one pleases, provided that a sense, and a precise one, is given to them. We insist only on distinguishing between serious metaphysical inquiry and verbiage disguised as such.

I have used the word 'metaphysics'; and I know that the suggestion that metaphysics is done at Oxford will meet with some incredulity. But this is largely due to a terminological muddle. We *do* metaphysics at Oxford; but we *call* it something else – usually 'logic' in an eccentrically wide sense of the word. In philosophy examinations at Oxford, the paper to which perhaps more attention is paid than to any other in assessing the merits of candidates is called 'Logic'; but it includes many questions which would be called in other places metaphysical. There are, for example, questions about time and space and their nature; about substance; about the nature of universals, and so on; as well as more narrowly logical questions. The title of the paper is traditional, and dates from long before the rise of the analytical movement; but although this nomenclature may be due to fortuitous historical causes, it serves to draw attention to an age-old difficulty in making a distinction between logic and metaphysics.

Metaphysics began when Socrates refused to answer first-order questions about, for example, what things are right, before he had had a satisfactory answer to second-order questions such as 'What is rightness?' This refusal was called by Plato 'demanding, in the case of everything, a definition (or account) of what-it-is-to-be that thing, or of its essential being (λόγον ἑκάστου λαμβάνειν τῆς οὐσίας)', and was said by him to be the mark of the true dialectical philosopher.[1] Aristotle's *Metaphysics* is centred round a study of this Socratic question, and may be regarded as a third-order inquiry – an inquiry, not into what-it-is-to-be any *particular* kind of thing, but into the very concept *what-it-is-to-be* something (τὸ τί ἦν εἶναί τινι, οὐσία). That is why it is called a study of being *qua* being (τὸ ὂν ᾗ ὄν). In more modern terms, Socrates would not have words used before an account was given of their meaning; Plato said that this attitude was characteristic of the philosopher, and Aristotle tried to give a general account of what it was philosophers were after. At that time, and ever since, the ordinary man has found something trifling about such second- and third-order enquiries: 'Trivial disputes about words!' say the enemies of modern philosophy; 'Abstract and metaphysical questions divorced from reality!' has always been the cry of those who do not like philosophers. Even at the very beginning, Aristophanes attacked Socrates for occupying himself with trivial verbal questions,[2] and no doubt Plato's *Cratylus*, in the eyes of the

---

[1] *Republic*, 534 b.   [2] *Clouds*, 659 ff.

ordinary man, lent colour to the accusation. We at Oxford, who in England are the chief butt of such attacks, are content to be the successors of Socrates, Plato and Aristotle, the study of whose philosophies remains a large part of our syllabus; we do not think it a trivial matter that people should understand what they are saying.

But it is a great deal easier to say what Oxford philosophers are not, than to say what they are. First of all, the philosophy which we practise bears only a historical relation to the so-called 'Logical Positivism' or 'Logical Empiricism' of the Vienna Circle. It is true that we at Oxford, unlike most German philosophers, find it easy to discuss philosophical questions with those who have remained more faithful to the traditions of Vienna. But the explanation of this is not hard to find. The Vienna Circle made certain apparently very damaging criticisms of the kind of philosophy that was current in their day. In Oxford, and in England generally, we have taken those criticisms seriously, and have, indeed, produced a whole new way of doing philosophy in the course of finding answers to them. We therefore share with the critics a basis of discussion such as neither of us shares with those who have chosen to ignore these important developments and to carry on in their old ways as if nothing had happened. For example, although very few of us would assent to the old 'Verification Theory of Meaning', we have recognised the necessity of developing a comprehensive theory of meaning to take its place,[1] and we therefore find it hard to discuss philosophy with, or to read the books of, people who do not seem to be *worried* about the problem of convincing the sceptic that their philosophical propositions mean something.

It would be incorrect, even, to tie to us, without qualification, the label 'Empiricists' – a label which gets almost automatically affixed to the English by Continental philosophers. For we practise a radical methodological scepticism with regard to the meaningfulness or usefulness of *all* these old philosophical labels. An empiricist is a person, presumably, who believes that all knowledge springs from experience. But what is 'knowledge'? What is 'experience'? What is it for knowledge to 'spring from'

[1] A very good introduction to modern discussions about meaning is Professor Ryle's article 'The Theory of Meaning' in *British Philosophy in the Mid-Century*, ed. C. A. Mace.

experience? As soon as we ask ourselves these questions, we are afflicted by doubts, which we seek to resolve by asking ourselves, 'How did we find ourselves using these terms?' So we go back over the ground that philosophy has covered, trying to pick up the trail of significance. The trail undoubtedly started from common language. Plato, for example, had no technical vocabulary to start with; and we cannot understand what he may have meant by a word like *eidos* without studying how, in the dialogues, he introduces the term and gives it a use.[1] But his explanations are always, and have to be, made in terms of ordinary words of Greek common speech; and if we are to understand the philosophy of Plato, or of anybody who takes over Plato's philosophical apparatus, it is absolutely necessary to make sure that, in passing from ordinary uses of words to their technical uses, they have not parted company with sense. In general our reaction, when confronted with a piece of philosophical diction, is to demand that the words in it be given a definite and unambiguous use.

This is not to say that for us the terms of common speech (in Greek, English, or any other language) are themselves above suspicion. We are not, as has been often suggested, uncritical worshippers of common speech; nor do we insist that all philosophy must be expressed in common speech – though obviously it would be an advantage if it could be. Apart from the fact that many common words have a philosophical origin (for example, 'cause', 'accident' and 'quality'), the most that we can know from the fact that the word has a use in common speech is that it has a use; *what* precisely its use may be, or whether it has more than one use, easily confused with one another, or whether its use is quite different in kind from expressions of apparently similar grammatical form – these are questions which require a very careful investigation of the actual use of expressions. There is no sure way of avoiding being deceived by words, except to pay very careful attention to words – that is one reason why the accusation that 'linguistic philosophers' are likely to take the linguistic form for the

[1] Oxford is one of the few places where ancient philosophy is studied, in Greek, as part of the philosophical curriculum, under tutors who have both an up-to-date philosophical training and a thorough classical education. In most other universities one may study Plato either in Greek but not as a philosopher, or as a philosopher but in translation.

philosophical reality is the very reverse of the truth. A few Oxford philosophers are so impressed by these difficulties that they concentrate on a systematic mapping of the categories and conceptual apparatus of common language, whether or not philosophical problems have yet arisen concerning them. These philosophers are far from denying the value of other sorts of philosophical enquiry, but are convinced of the usefulness of such a basic study as a foundation for philosophy. The majority, however, are content to go on investigating those problems which are by common consent called philosophical – but investigating them with at least one eye fixed on the need for knowing, all the time, precisely what one is saying. These two kinds of study are of great assistance to each other; the relation between them is similar to that between geologists who prospect for minerals and those who seek to advance our systematic knowledge of the subject.

It is frequently said of the so-called 'linguistic philosophers' that, through concentrating their attention on words and their meanings, they have abandoned the study of 'the world' or of 'reality'. This accusation reveals a curious misconception about what a *word* is. There is, I suppose, a sense of the word 'word' in which, if I were to cut out of the page of a book a piece of paper carefully chosen as to position, what I should have would be a word. *This* could be studied without studying any more of reality than the piece of inky paper. Perhaps, even, there are certain aspects of linguistic studies which do not involve any consideration of meanings. If so, they have little to do with philosophy – even 'linguistic philosophy'. But philosophers are concerned with words as having meanings or uses; and these at any rate cannot be studied without seeing how words are used, in concrete situations, to say various things; and, of course, this involves (as is evident from our practice) a careful study of the situations, in order to find out what is being said. Thus, the philosopher who asks what is meant by saying 'I intend to kill him' has to ask himself how this expression would, concretely, be used; and this involves a study of more than pieces of inky paper. A full philosophical examination of language would involve a full examination of everything that can be talked about – and if there are things that cannot be talked about, they cannot in any case become the subject of a philosophical enquiry.

It is sometimes said that if the philosopher studies words, he will get caught in the meshes of his own language – English or whatever it may be. Now, the fact that a thing can be said in any particular language is sufficient proof that it can be said – and this may be of philosophical interest. In so far as the same thing can be exactly translated into some other language, the philosophical results established in terms of the first language will be statable in the second language. How far various sentences in the two languages are equivalent to one another is a philological, not a philosophical question (though it is an interesting philosophical question, what we mean by saying that they are equivalent). It is of interest to the philosopher, however, if some foreign language can be used to say things that cannot be said in his own. For example, the fact that to the English expression 'I could have' there correspond in Latin two expressions, *potui* and *potuissem*, which have different meanings, has been used by Professor Austin to bring out an important and unsuspected ambiguity in the English expression, which has far-reaching implications for the study of the problem of moral responsibility.[1] One can also *coin* expressions if they do not exist in one's own language (though one must be careful to give them a meaning); and this to some extent exempts the philosopher from an exhaustive search for logical specimens in foreign languages. One can *experiment* with language. If one is successful in giving sense to a newly coined form of expression, that, too, proves something. So the philosopher who uses and studies no language but his own is not necessarily the prisoner of that language's conceptual structure. But knowledge of other languages can provide important stimuli to enquiry – stimuli which are certainly not lacking in Oxford.

And so the subject-matter of 'linguistic philosophy' is not, after all, clearly divided from the subject-matters of other sorts of philosophy. 'Linguistic philosophy' is simply philosophy, but done with a proper awareness of the pitfalls of language, which others ignore, and a determination to avoid these pitfalls, both by carefully charting those which have been discovered, and by keeping a good look-out for any uncharted ones that there may be. Nor have philosophers at Oxford any obvious common tenets. If one took any of the well-known controversies

[1] 'Ifs and Cans', *Proceedings of the British Academy*, XLII (1956) 109. Reprinted in J. L. Austin, *Philosophical Papers*, p. 164.

in philosophy, such as that between the realists and nominalists, or that between objectivism and subjectivism in ethics, and asked a lot of Oxford philosophers what they thought, they would probably agree in rejecting as inadequate or unclear all of the best-known formulations of either side in these controversies. But this would be likely to be the full extent of their agreement; they would be sure to dispute hotly with one another about the correct way of resolving the problems. The most obvious common characteristic of Oxford philosophers is, indeed, their propensity for arguing with one another – here is one place in the world, at any rate, where people holding opposing views on philosophical problems can meet and understand one another's arguments – and this presupposes, first that Oxford philosophers seldom agree, but secondly that they have sufficient confidence in the rigour and honesty and clarity of each other's thought to hope that argument will not be a waste of time. In fact, what we share are not tenets but standards (which we may or may not live up to, but go on trying); Oxford, that is to say, is not so much a school of philosophy as a school for philosophers.

4 A Question about Plato's Theory of Ideas

A volume published in honour of Professor Popper would be incomplete without some contribution specifically intended to honour him as the writer of one of the very few recent books about Plato that are worth reading. Since Platonic scholarship, seriously pursued, can easily become a whole-time occupation, not many philosophers have been prepared to leave their main field of interest, even temporarily, in order to raise historical questions about the beginnings of their subject. Yet unless they do so, Platonic studies will lose contact with Plato the philosopher. Unless he is studied, at least sometimes, by those whose main interest is in the philosophical questions which he and his master Socrates first raised, scholars will be left in a position not unlike that of historians trying to piece together Hannibal's route from ancient sources without taking a look at the Alps. I make no apology, therefore, for following Popper's example, but only for my lack of equipment for the task.

The most useful contribution that philosophers can make to Platonic studies is to ask questions in the hope that specialist scholars may find the answers. I wish in this paper to ask one such question. It is a question which is extremely hard to make clear, and to distinguish from other apparently similar questions. I shall therefore go further, and suggest a tentative answer to it, and even consider what light is shed on the question by the text of the dialogues; but I do this only in order to clarify the question as that question to which this answer is an appropriate (though possibly a false) one. The major task remains of attempting to test this hypothesis by an exhaustive study of the textual and other evidence. This enormous task I

Excerpted, with minor corrections, from *The Critical Approach: Essays in Honor of Karl Popper*, ed. Mario Bunge (Free Press of Glencoe, 1964). Original version © 1964 by The Free Press of Glencoe, Illinois.

have barely begun; one of the purposes of publishing this paper is to enlist help in it. All that can be said is that I have failed so far to find much evidence which seems to tell against the hypothesis, and that even this may admit of alternative explanations. I have, however, found quite compelling evidence, as it seems to me, against some alternative hypotheses. With the object, therefore, of presenting a clear-cut proposal for discussion, I shall argue the case for my suggested answer with greater apparent confidence than I in fact feel.

My question, it must be emphasised, is not a philosophical one, and no answer to it should contain any philosophical terminology – though a good deal of philosophy will be required in order to distinguish this question from others. Nor is it a question of exegesis. It is a historical question of a psychological sort. That is to say, I am not going to ask, either what Plato may have meant by certain things that he said, or whether he was right. To answer either of these questions would require at the outset a statement in philosophical terms of certain propositions to which, in my view, Plato would have assented. But I shall not be discussing at all (except in passing) what were or were not Plato's philosophical views. What I want to know (because it has a crucial bearing on many philosophical and exegetical questions about Plato) is the answer to a plain question of psychological fact: What, in certain circumstances and on certain occasions which I shall specify, was actually going on in Plato's experience ? The circumstances and occasions in question are, roughly, those in which Plato himself would have said 'I am seeing (or apprehending) an Idea'.[1] The answer to this question must be couched in terms which would enable us, if the same thing happened in our own experience, to recognise it and say 'That was the sort of thing that Plato was referring to when he said . . ., etc.' It is therefore necessary that the answer to the question should be given in words which we can all understand – and in particular, not in philosophical language. Since my question is not a philosophical one, I can demand an answer to it in plain English without incurring any of Popper's strictures against 'ordinary-language philosophy'.

[1] The difference between 'seeing' Ideas and 'apprehending' them is no doubt important, since to see a bird is very different from catching it; but I shall have no room to deal with this distinction.

I

I will now illustrate the character of my question by asking
another question which is of just the same kind, but to which the
answer is fairly obvious. Suppose that we were to ask, in the
context of *Republic* VI and VII, what was actually happening in
Plato's experience when he was doing what he calls '*eikasiâ*'.
This word is one of the four key terms which Plato uses in
expounding his theory of knowledge in these books, in the simile
known as 'The Line'. The other three are called in 511 d
'*pistis*', '*dianoiâ*' and '*noêsis*' – though '*noêsis*' is later used
generically to include *dianoiâ* (534 a).

In 511 d it is said that these four 'experiences in the mind
(*pathêmata en têi psŷchêi*)' have as their objects four kinds of
thing, which have been described earlier. *Eikasiâ* has as its
objects 'shadows, and reflections in water and in anything that
is fine-textured and smooth and shiny, and so forth'; and *pistis*
has as its objects 'the animals in our environment and the entire
classes of plants and of man-made objects' (510 a). From this
it is clear that when Plato was engaging in *eikasiâ* he was looking
at, e.g., a reflection in water, and that when he was engaging in
pistis he was looking at, e.g., a horse or a table. It is this kind
of answer that we require to the question, 'What was Plato
doing when he was engaging in *dianoiâ* or *noêsis*?' We all
sometimes look at horses, tables and reflections in water; and
therefore, when Plato mentions these activities, or experiences,
we all know to what he is alluding. We need to know in just
the same way to what sort of experience he is alluding when he
talks about seeing or apprehending Ideas (which, as we learn
from 511 c and elsewhere, are the objects of *noêsis*). We need to
be able to catch ourselves doing (if we ever do) what Plato
describes in these terms; for if we cannot do this, we shall never
be able to understand all the further things which he says
about this activity. We do not, however, need to accept all
these further things in order to be able to identify, in our own
experience, that activity about which he is saying them.

The distinction between identifying the experience and
understanding the philosophical things which are said about
the experience will perhaps become clearer if we consider
what we should say to a person who answered, to our question

about *eikasiâ*, that when Plato was doing this he was 'having sense-data'. If no importance is being attached, in this answer, to the difference, if any, between the experience (whatever it is) called 'having sense-data' and the experience called 'looking at a shadow or reflection', then, indeed, this answer becomes a somewhat affected way of expressing the correct answer, namely that Plato was looking at a shadow or reflection. But if, on the other hand, some importance *is* being attached to the alleged difference between having sense-data and looking at a shadow or reflection, then the answer becomes either inapposite or wrong. For if the difference between having sense-data and looking at a shadow or reflection is an empirical one, then, since 'Plato was looking at a shadow or reflection' is the correct answer to the question 'What experience was Plato having?', 'Plato was having sense-data' must be an incorrect answer, since the two experiences are, on this supposition, different ones. If, on the other hand, the difference is not an empirical one, but a difference between two philosophical theories about the same experience, then the answer is inapposite – an answer to the wrong question, for the question asked was not what philosophical theories Plato had about this experience, but what the experience was.

We want, therefore, an answer to the question 'What was happening in Plato's experience when he was, as he would have put it, "seeing or apprehending an Idea"?' which is like the answer 'Plato was looking at a shadow or reflection' and not like the answer 'Plato was having sense-data'. We must, accordingly, rule out from the start, as not being answers (even wrong answers) to our question, such suggestions as 'Plato was intuiting a transcendental universal'. For while it may be true that this is what Plato, if we could ask him, and if he knew the English of the schools, would say as a philosopher about the experience in question, such an 'answer' does absolutely nothing to help us identify the experience which is the subject of this philosophical pronouncement. For how are we to know when we are doing this thing called 'intuiting a transcendental universal', and when we are not? To answer to our question 'Plato was intuiting a transcendental universal' is therefore no more illuminating than to answer 'Plato was *noón*, or *pros tên ideán blepôn*' (or one of the other ways in which he puts it). We want to know what was happening.

E

II

Now a possible, and indeed plausible, answer to our question would be the disappointing one that no single thing was happening on all the occasions on which Plato would have said he was seeing or apprehending an Idea. It might be that a great many different things were happening on different occasions, and that he failed to distinguish them. Perhaps, however, it is not necessary to be as pessimistic as this. For even though it would be surprising if it could be shown that on *every* occasion of which Plato would have spoken in these terms the same thing was going on in his experience, we ought perhaps to be content with the lesser satisfaction of discovering that *in paradigm or typical cases* a certain kind of thing was happening, and that Plato's theory was an attempt to assimilate the less elementary and more interesting cases to these paradigm cases. This would be a temptation into which many philosophers have fallen.

We have, however, at the outset to answer a possible objection to our procedure of looking for something in our own experience which might be similar to what was going on in Plato's when he would have said he was looking at an Idea. This would be a vain search, if Plato, when he was 'looking at an Idea', was having a very high-grade mystical experience such as we ordinary mortals cannot aspire to. But fortunately this suggestion runs counter to some quite strong evidence in the dialogues. For while it is true that Plato does sometimes speak of apprehending certain of the Ideas as a matter of great difficulty requiring the highest powers of intellect, he speaks at others as if the simpler Ideas were open to inspection by the meanest minds. We learn from *Rep.* 596 b and *Crat.* 389 a that a carpenter (who would have been in the lowest class in Plato's city) looks at the relevant Idea every time he makes a table or a bed or a shuttle. It is also implied by the Plato–Diogenes story (see below) that Plato thought that anybody who cannot see the Ideas of Cup and Table has, to say the least, a low I.Q. As we shall see, Plato thought that some Ideas were more difficult to apprehend than others; and it may also be true that, until the highest Idea, that of the Good, was apprehended, he thought that there was something lacking in our *knowledge* even of the lower ones which depended upon it (*Rep.* 511 c, d).

And we must not assume that Plato thought that ordinary carpenters (any more than ordinary mathematicians) could give a *logos* or definition of the Ideas with which they were concerned – to this extent they lacked knowledge or art (*epistêmê, technê*), for which the ability to give a *logos* is a necessary condition (*Rep.* 510 c, 533 c; *Meno* 98 a; *Gorg.* 465 a).

But when all this is said, it remains true that, according to Plato, ordinary men could look at and see the simpler Ideas, even if it took a philosopher to make them attend to what they were seeing. Anybody, therefore, who has ever made a table can properly ask, 'Which, of all the things that I did when making it, corresponds to what Plato said the carpenter was doing when he was "looking at the Idea" ?'

III

It will be helpful, however, if we start our search, not among the carpenters, about whom Plato tells us too little, but among the mathematicians, about whom he tells us a lot, though obscurely. In *Rep.* 510 d he says of them, among other things, that they

> use, in addition, visible forms (*eidê*) [as diagrams], and talk about them, though it is not about them that they are thinking (*dianooumenoi*), but rather about those other [Forms] whose likenesses they are. Thus, the object of their discussion is the Square itself, and the Diagonal itself, not this diagonal which they scratch on the sand; and so with the rest of the figures. These scratched or handmade things which have as we saw *their* likenesses – shadows and reflections in water – are themselves, in their turn, used by the mathematicians as likenesses (*eikones*) when they are trying to see those things-themselves, which are not to be seen with anything but the mind.

It is not certain that here 'the Square itself' is an Idea; but those who have argued that it is have, besides good general grounds, support in the text of this passage: there is the familiar wording, 'the Square itself', echoed later in the phrase 'those other things-themselves'; and it is surely correct, as it certainly is natural, to supply the noun '*tôn eidôn*', understood, after 'those other' in the fourth line of the quotation – indeed,

the opportunity for this veiled allusion to his technical term
may be the reason for Plato's use of the otherwise rather odd
expression 'visible *eidé*' for mathematical diagrams.

However this may be, it is hard to deny that the language
which Plato uses in speaking of the mathematicians' dealings
with 'the Square itself' is entirely typical of the sort of language
which he generally uses in speaking of our dealings with Ideas.
We may notice in particular that the Square itself and the
Diagonal itself are the objects of their discussion (*logoi*) and that
they are trying to 'see them . . . with the mind'. From this
language it is at any rate clear that 'the Square itself' is not
any kind of talk, mental or otherwise, but rather something
that is talked about; and it seems that 'making it the object of
their discussion' (literally 'making their discourse for the sake
of it') is a different activity from actually seeing it, since the
mathematicians are already doing the former, but only trying
to do the latter. They are trying to see it with an organ called
'mind' (*dianoiâ*); and this visual language is repeated later
(511 c), where it is applied equally to the higher activity
called *noêsis*, which is indisputably concerned with Ideas.

From the use of words for seeing, in connection both with
dianoiâ and with *noêsis*, throughout the two 'Line' passages, it
is clear that, whatever may be the differences between the two
upper segments of the Line,[1] the activities which they represent
both consist, in part, in some sort of *seeing* which is not the
seeing of ordinary visible objects with the eyes, but the seeing
of something else by the use of some other faculty. And indeed
the whole of this part of the *Republic*, and especially the simile
of the Sun (508 ff.), is full of this metaphor (if Plato thought
of it as a metaphor) of seeing; and he constantly seems to
envisage that faculty with which we do our thinking – or at
any rate the best and proper kind of thinking – as 'the eye of
the mind' (533 d). This is the point of the story told by Diogenes
Laertius about an encounter between his namesake the Cynic
and Plato (6,2,53; for another version, with Antisthenes
instead of Diogenes, see Simplicius, *ad Arist. Cat.* 66 b, 67 b).
Diogenes, poking fun at the Theory of Ideas, said, 'I see the
table and the cup; but *tableness* and *cupness* – I can't see *them*
at all'; to which Plato replied, 'Of course; because the cup
and the table are seen with the eyes, which you have; but

[1] For these, see the following essay.

tableness and cupness are seen with the *nous*, which you lack.'

This assimilation of thinking to a kind of mental seeing had a past and was to have a future. In Homer the verb *noein* (with which *nous*, *dianoiá* and *noêsis* are all cognate) is used both of visual perception (*Il.* 15, 422) and of 'noticing' consequent upon such perception (*Il.* 11, 599) and of pure thought (*Il.* 19, 112). The future of the comparison is testified to by the passage into philosophical terminology of the words 'theory' and 'intuition' (both derived from words for looking); but we must be careful not to be misled, through our familiarity with the watered-down meaning which these terms now bear, into thinking that the comparison was not conceived of by Plato as a very exact one.

IV

Let us now recur to our original problem. If we make the working assumption that Plato's mental processes were not entirely unlike our own, the evidence which we have so far noticed suggests a possible answer. Speaking very roughly and crudely, what we do when we are thinking may be classified into, first, talking to ourselves, and secondly, the forming of 'mental images'.[1] In the latter we must include, not only quasi-visual images, but also imagined sounds, smells, etc.; and it is perhaps necessary to include also the feelings which may be associated with these images – as when someone imagines a pretty girl and experiences the feeling called 'lust'. This classification is, I repeat, crude; but it may be exact enough to deal with Plato's first attempts to give an account of thinking.

Of these two kinds of thinking, it has already become apparent, and will shortly become even more so, that Plato is not equating the 'seeing' of Ideas with the first, namely talking to oneself – although in the *Sophist* he does describe thinking (*dianoiá*) as 'the discourse of the mind with itself' (263 e). For he generally speaks as if the talking that we do, to ourselves or others, were not itself the seeing of the Ideas but something that was *about* the objects of this seeing, in order to assist the talker to 'see' them, or show that he had 'seen' them. It seems to

[1] Aristotle held that 'there is no thought without a mental image' (*De An.* 431 a16; cf. 432 a8); the interpretation of this is, however, doubtful.

follow, by elimination, that what was happening when Plato was 'seeing' an Idea was something falling within the vague class 'the forming of mental images'. And it seems fair, if anyone doubts this, to ask him what else he thinks could have been happening.

Consider, now, the famous passage in the Seventh Letter (342 a) in which are discussed 'the necessary conditions of knowledge'. Even if Plato did not himself write this letter, it is probably near enough to him in time to be of some use as evidence; and it contains the fullest list available of the things that are, in the Platonic view, involved in knowledge. Three things are listed: the name of the thing known, e.g. 'circle'; its definition (*logos*), e.g. 'the figure whose circumference is everywhere equidistant from the centre'; and what is called the 'image (*eidôlon*)'. By this latter, it is said, is meant 'that which is drawn and rubbed out and turned on a lathe and broken' – i.e. what we should call a physical object or diagram. Plato often speaks of physical objects as 'images' or 'likenesses' of Ideas. And this is no doubt the main reason why the answer to our problem which I have proposed seems at first sight scandalous. The answer is, however, once it is properly understood, no cause for scandal at all. For I am not suggesting that Plato equated his Ideas with any mental images. He, it goes without saying, would have dissented from this identification, because to call something a mental image is, in our way of speaking, to deny that it is a real thing (in the ordinary sense of those words), whereas Plato wanted to attribute the highest kind of reality to what he said he was seeing. This, however, is part of the philosophical interpretation of the experience, and therefore has no bearing on our problem; what is being suggested is that the experience which Plato, interpreting it one way, would have called 'seeing an idea', we, interpreting it another way, would call 'forming a mental image'. We shall later recur to this distinction.

Once this misunderstanding is cleared away, the use of the words 'image' and 'likeness' of physical objects and diagrams actually supports the suggested answer. For it is of the essence of an image or likeness to be like the object imaged; and since similarity is a symmetrical relation (cf. *Parm.* 132 d), the object must also be like the image. Therefore, if Plato attributed the highest sort of reality to what we would call 'a mental image', it was very natural to him to call the physical object an 'image' or 'likeness' of it, instead of the other way round. Since there is nothing so like a physical object, in one way, as the mental image of it, it is obvious that 'forming a mental image' is a much better candidate for the position of what Plato was doing when he was, in his terms, 'seeing an Idea' than, for example, is 'holding mental discourse with himself'.

But the passage in the Seventh Letter affords much more positive evidence than this. After listing the three things just mentioned (name, definition, image) the Letter adds two other things: the knowledge itself, and 'that which is the object of the knowledge, and which is in the true sense real' – sc. the Idea. Now since the Idea appears separately on this list, it cannot be identified with any other member of the list. Therefore it is not the name nor the *logos* or definition; nor is it, needless to say, the physical object, nor even the mental activity, knowledge, which consists in contemplating the Idea, though this activity, being mental (*en psychais*), is said to have the closest affinity with the Idea itself. We must ask, then, what else is left for the Idea to be but the object of this activity, i.e. that which is before the mind when one is engaged in it. And what could this be but a mental image, to which reality is ascribed by Plato? For with his (perhaps mistaken) conception of knowledge as – at least in part – an occurrent, i.e. not merely dispositional, activity analogous to sight, it is hard to see what other candidates there could be.

v

Further light is perhaps shed by a passage in Aristotle's *Metaphysics* (990 b8) in which he is attacking the Platonic version of the Theory of Ideas. 'None of the ways', he says, 'in which we show that there are Ideas are adequate to show this; for some of them do not necessarily lead to the desired conclusion, and some of them lead to Ideas of objects of which we do not think there are Ideas.' 'We' here means the Platonists, whose view Aristotle is in process of abandoning. He then lists a number of arguments, ending up with the following, which falls into the class 'ways which lead to Ideas of objects of which we do not think there are Ideas':

According to the argument, that we can think of an object when it has been destroyed, there will be Ideas of destructible objects; for there is a sort of mental image (*phantasma*) of these.

The argument referred to seems to have been somewhat similar to one recently revived by Professor Price, that 'thinking in absence' involves knowledge by acquaintance of universals.[1] The fact that we can think about an object after it has been destroyed means that what is before our mind cannot be the object itself; it must therefore be, say the Platonists, the Idea of the object. But, says Aristotle, this entails that there are Ideas of destructible objects – which, for some reason, he thinks would be repugnant to the position he is attacking. The fact that Aristotle here regards the existence of a mental image as requiring, for the Platonists, the existence of an Idea is support, of a kind, for our suggested answer to our problem, although, as we shall see, Aristotle was wrong if he thought that *whenever* Plato was having a mental image he would have said that he was seeing an Idea.

Consider next a passage which might be thought to tell against the suggested answer: *Parmenides* 132 b. Here Socrates, in order to avoid a difficulty which does not concern us, suggests that the Idea of each thing might be a thought (*noêma*), which cannot properly exist anywhere but 'in minds (*en psýchais*)'. Since this suggestion is firmly and summarily rejected by Parmenides, and does not recur, it is safe to assume that Plato did not think it a good one. It might therefore be argued that whatever else the Ideas were, they cannot have been mental images, which are also, in some sense, 'in minds'. But to argue thus is to misunderstand, in a way against which I have been at great pains to warn the reader, both the question which we are asking and the suggested answer. Plato's language here is perfectly consistent with the theory that what was happening when Plato said 'I am seeing an Idea' was what *we* should describe as 'Plato having a mental image', though it is inconsistent with the theory, if anyone held it, that Plato would *himself* have said 'The Ideas are mental images'. That is to say, the passage tells against the view that Plato would have accepted an utterly un-Platonic philosophical interpretation of

[1] *Thinking and Experience*, pp. 103 ff.

what was happening, but not against our suggestion about what *was* happening.

Let us, however, examine the argument a little more closely. The word '*noêma*' clearly means, as Cornford says, not 'object of thought' but 'act of thinking'. The first argument of Parmenides against the suggestion that the Ideas are acts of thinking (the only argument that concerns us) is that there cannot be an act of thought without an object of thought, and this is the Idea. Here the same distinction is made as in the Seventh Letter between a mental activity and its object. Thus this passage supports rather than conflicts with our suggested answer. When Plato was having a mental image, he thought of what was happening as follows. He, Plato, was, as it were, seeing something, and that which he was seeing might be an Idea – that is to say, a real universal object of thought (though it might equally well not be an Idea – hence the need for the *elenchus* and all the other apparatus for sifting genuine from spurious objects of thought). This view entailed that, at least, one could take another look at this Idea on another occasion, and it would be the same thing that one was looking at. But the fact that Plato thought of his experience in this way does not mean that what was actually happening was anything other than that for which the correct English description is 'Plato having a mental image'.

A parallel from modern philosophy (already briefly alluded to) may perhaps make the situation clearer. There is no experimental difference, it is sometimes said, between seeing a table and having tablish visual sense-data. But there are two ways of talking about this experience, called 'sense-datum language' and 'material-object language', of which the former carries much weaker implications than the latter. If I say 'I see a table', I imply, for example, that others can have similar or related experiences, and that I can at a future time myself 'see the same table again'. But (according to sense-datum theorists) if I say 'I am having tablish sense-data', I imply nothing about any other experience that I or somebody else might have. Plato's proposal, on the suggestion that I have made, could be put in the following way: he was proposing that we should start using material-object language about some of our mental images (for all of which we now use a kind of sense-datum language) and, perhaps, that we should start using a sense-datum type of language in speaking of what we now call material objects (though Plato is far from actually carrying out the latter proposal, for all that it is strongly suggested by his talk about *doxa* that this is what he really wanted to do). Thus material objects are no longer to be called 'real' (because one cannot step into the same river twice); and those mental images which pass muster are to be treated as independently existing objects, available to repeated inspection by different people, and called 'truly real'. There seems to be at any rate no *greater* logical difficulty in talking like this than there would be in adopting a sense-datum language when speaking about tables (though both proposals are probably misguided). The adoption of a new language would not in either case make any difference to the experiences that were being had. The sense-datum theorists and Plato are both making suggestions about how we should speak, but the experiences about which they are speaking are the same experiences as we have learnt to recognise and to describe in quite different terms.

VI

We must next ask whether the suggested answer to our question will fit the whole of 'the population of the world of Ideas'.[1] For if there is any class of things of which it is impossible to form mental images, but of which Plato did admit Ideas, that would be evidence against the suggestion that I have made, unless it could be shown that, though it is in fact impossible to form mental images of these things, Plato did not recognise this impossibility. It will not be sufficient, in order to refute the suggestion, to show that we *actually* cannot form mental images of a class of things of which Plato admitted Ideas. For it may be that he thought that, by strenuous philosophical endeavour, he might come to be able to do what we would call 'having a mental image of these things', and he would call 'seeing the Ideas of them'. In any case, it is not to be expected, even if the answer which I have proposed is the right one, that it will fit all kinds of Ideas equally well. I suggested earlier that

---

[1] This phrase is borrowed from Sir David Ross's book *Plato's Theory of Ideas*, to which, in spite of disagreements, my debt is obvious.

what Plato might have been doing was to assimilate the more difficult cases to his paradigm cases. If this were so, then we should expect to find some cases which fit in quite easily, and others which present greater difficulty; and we should also expect to find Plato giving evidence that in these latter cases he finds difficulties which he does not find in the easier ones.

The cases which fit in most easily are the simpler geometrical ones. Do we not all quite frequently, when thinking about the properties of the circle or the square, form to ourselves a mental image of a circle or a square, and think about the properties of this? Now it will, of course, be said that the mental image that we form is still, like a physical diagram, particular, and therefore can have nothing to do with what Plato was referring to. But is this so obvious? What would be the *experimental* difference between forming a particular image of a square, and mentally seeing the universal, the Square, on a particular occasion? Or between forming a number of particular images of particular squares at different times, and seeing, on a number of particular occasions, the one universal called 'the Square'? If it be thought – as it is easy to think – that there is no experiential difference, it is not difficult to see how Plato can have interpreted the experience which *we* call 'having a particular mental image of a square' as 'having, on a particular occasion, a mental look at the Square'. It is true that one can look *simultaneously* at two imagined squares, whereas there could not be two Ideas of the Square; but this difficulty, which led to Plato's invention of the 'mathematicals', probably did not occur to him until quite late in life; that it was, when noticed, felt as a difficulty is some evidence in favour of our suggestion.

The mental image, considered in this way, has many of the qualifications that Plato was obviously looking for in his search for reality. It is always available for inspection; it is independent of the chances and changes of the world, not being, as physical images are, drawn and then rubbed out. The mental image, it is true, vanishes when we turn our attention to something else; but Plato may have thought that, although we were no longer looking at it, it was still there to be looked at. Moreover, once one has come to look upon the experience which we call having mental images as looking at a transcendental reality, it is extremely tempting to think of physical squares and circles as images of the mental ones and not vice versa, since, as we have already seen and as Plato himself pointed out, the relation of similarity is a symmetrical one. That is why mathematical diagrams are said to be 'images' or 'likenesses' of the Square and the Circle. On any other theory, how can these words be called in the least appropriate ?

It is not necessary, therefore, to look for any more complicated explanations of *Republic* 510 d ff. (the passage first discussed) than that suggested by the text. What the mathematicians are doing is, in our own terms, drawing diagrams on the sand, and talking (apparently) about them, but trying to form a mental image of a square and a diagonal and to discover their properties (a process which Plato describes, not as we have, but as 'trying to see those things-themselves, which are not to be seen with anything but the mind').

It cannot be denied that Plato was here starting a great deal more than he was aware of. No doubt, once one has realised that geometry discovers universal truths and not truths about particular objects, one has started on a journey which does not end until one arrives at analytical geometry and dispenses with figures of all sorts, both physical and mental. Geometry then becomes a branch of algebra, and thus, according to some logicians, of logic. There are indications in Plato's account, in his talk about dialectic in the *Republic* and about *logoi* there and elsewhere, of the direction which the journey was to take. All I am denying is that Plato had, when he wrote the *Republic*, got as far on this journey as some people have supposed. Philosophical advances are much more difficult to make than often appears after they have been made. It is one of the commonest sources of error in interpreting Plato to suppose that, being a great philosopher, he must have seen what is obvious to us. But these things are obvious to us only because pioneer philosophers – of whom, though Plato was one of the greatest, there have been others since – have discovered them and made them part of the common body of knowledge which is the despised inheritance of every schoolboy. No doubt it is obvious to us that the easiest way of conveying heavy loads is on wheels; but that does not mean that the man who first thought of conveying them on rollers was stupid.

There is one particular logical objection to thinking as, on my view, Plato did, and this might also be advanced as an objection to thinking that he thought in this way – for no admirer of Plato likes to suppose him guilty of not having thought of everything. This is the objection raised by Berkeley (*Principles*, Introd., 13) against Locke (*Essay* IV, 7, 9). Locke has said that one must form an idea of a triangle which is 'neither oblique nor rectangle, neither equilateral nor equicrural nor scalenon, but all and none of these at once'; and Berkeley said that this is manifestly impossible – as indeed it is, if one means by 'idea of a triangle' what Berkeley, and perhaps also Locke, meant by it. Berkeley's objection could be raised against Plato too, if Plato was thinking as I have suggested. One cannot form a mental image of a triangle which is neither equilateral nor equicrural nor scalenon; and therefore, when Plato was 'seeing the Idea of the Triangle', he would have, on my view, to have been doing the impossible.

There is, in fact, a passage in the *Meno* (74 d ff.) in which Plato uses words which are very reminiscent of Locke. Socrates is discussing the definition of Shape (*schêma*); and, quoting the words of an imaginary questioner, with whom he is in sympathy, he says, 'Since you call these many things by one name, and say that every one of them is a shape, though they are, even, opposite to one another' (he has been discussing the shapes called 'curved' and 'straight') 'will you not say that there is this thing that comprises the curved no less than the straight, which you call "shape" ?' And the Idea of Colour, which is dealt with in the same passage, presents a similar difficulty.

Now it is possible that Locke meant by 'idea' what Berkeley probably thought he meant, viz. 'mental image'. In this case Berkeley's criticism of Locke is justified; but we can then argue that, if Locke, writing with more than two thousand years of philosophical history behind him, could make the mistake of thinking that one can form mental images having incompatible characteristics, so may Plato have. If this were so, the possibility of this objection being raised does not make it impossible that Plato should have failed to notice it; and so the possibility of the objection is not conclusive evidence against the answer to our problem which I have suggested. On the other hand, it is possible that Berkeley was misunderstanding Locke, and that Locke did not mean by 'idea', 'mental image'. In this case, Locke may have been right in thinking that it is possible, though difficult, to form an idea of a triangle having these incompatible characteristics – though in that case the difficult question remains, 'In what sense *was* Locke using the word "idea" ?' If, however, we let Locke escape in this way, we can argue that, since *Berkeley* could have been confused on this point, so may Plato have been. This is, indeed, one of the most confusing topics in philosophy, and it would be surprising if either Plato or Locke or Berkeley were entirely clear about it – I certainly am not.

In any case, even if the argument of the preceding paragraph be not accepted, there is a shorter way with this objection. For it would apply to any view which held that, for Plato, the Idea of the Triangle was a triangle, whether or not my 'mental image' suggestion is a sound one. And (though this has been disputed) it seems certain in the light of passages like *Phaedo* 74 that Plato did accept the thesis of 'self-predication' – viz. that the Ideas themselves possessed the qualities of which they were Ideas.[1] If so, the Idea of the Triangle will have to be some sort of triangle; and so the question 'Is it equilateral, etc., or all, or none of these things ?' will arise. Since, therefore, the Berkeley objection arises for Plato whatever the truth of my contentions, it is easiest to suppose that he had not noticed that he was open to it.

There is a further possibility to be considered, which I suggest with great diffidence, since I have not yet had time to check it carefully against the text (which would require the close examination, with this specific question in mind, of all the dialogues). This is that the way of thinking which I have suggested was Plato's was only developed during the period of the middle dialogues, from which the most favourable examples seem to come. This was the period during which Plato appears often (though not always) to have taken 'imitation' as his model of the relation between Ideas and particular things; and this model fits in very well with the 'mental image' suggestion. In the earlier dialogues, perhaps, he was rather following Socrates in his search for definitions in words, and had not developed any 'Theory of Ideas' proper, in the sense that requires an answer to the question posed in this paper. If this were so, we should not be unduly disturbed to find, for example,

[1] See the illuminating series of articles in *Philosophical Review* (1954–60) initiated by Professor G. Vlastos (reprinted in *Studies in Plato's Metaphysics*, ed. R. E. Allen).

in the *Laches* (192 b), an early dialogue, a definition being given of Speed, of which it would be hard to form an image. The *Meno* might mark the transition from this stage to the fully developed theory. There is no reason to suppose that *Socrates* was trying to form mental images when he asked his 'What is . . . ?' questions; and therefore when we find him, in the early dialogues, asking and answering them about things which are scarcely imageable, this might be because the paradigm had for Plato not yet crystallised.

Another group of Ideas, already referred to, which fits our suggested answer very well is that of Ideas of manufactured objects. There is some evidence that at a later period Plato may have thought that there could not be such Ideas; but when he wrote the *Republic* and the *Cratylus* he certainly admitted them.[1] In general, Ideas of all concrete objects like horses, cups and tables present no difficulty; but in the case of manufactured objects in particular the suggestion is especially attractive. For if my experience is any guide, it is extremely common, when making something, first to form a mental image of the thing that one is going to make, and then copy the image. And this, translated into Platonic terms, is what Plato says the carpenter does when he makes a bed or a shuttle. 'Where does the carpenter look when he makes the shuttle ? Is it not at the sort of thing that has as its nature to fulfil the function of a shuttle ? . . . If the shuttle breaks as he is making it, will he, in making a replacement, look at the broken one, or will he look at that Idea (*eidos*) by reference to which he made also the one which he broke ?' (*Crat.* 389 a, b; cf. *Rep.* 596 b). Here it is significant that the carpenter is said to look at the Idea *and not* at the broken shuttle; presumably, therefore (since there is no hint of zeugma), the word 'look' is being used twice in very much the same sense; and this means that the way in which the carpenter looks at the Idea must be very like the way he might (though he does not) look at the broken shuttle. And it seems to be a plausible explanation of why Plato speaks in this way, that he thought that when the carpenter, as most carpenters do, visualises in his mind's eye the shuttle or table that he is going to make, he is actually seeing the Idea of the Shuttle or the Table. This explains both the attractiveness of the whole 'imitation' story in the *Republic* and elsewhere, and Plato's

[1] See Ross, op. cit., pp. 171 ff.

failure to distinguish between the ideal table (the standard example) and the property of being a table. For if one thinks that one tells whether a thing is an X by seeing whether it resembles the standard X which one can look at with one's mind's eye, then knowing what it is to be an X will be hard to distinguish from being able to summon up before one's mind's eye this ideal or standard X.

VII

When, however, we come to Ideas of more abstract notions, especially value-terms, the task of finding a mental image to correspond to them gets much more difficult. And this is just where, apparently, Plato himself began to find difficulty. In *Phaedrus* 263 a he says that, when anyone says the word 'iron' or 'silver', we all think (*dianoein*) the same thing; but when he says the words 'right' or 'good' then one man goes one way and one another. And among value-words some are easier than others.

> Righteousness and Good Behaviour and all the other admirable qualities of the mind have no earthly likenesses whose brightness picks them out; with our dull faculties we can see them only with difficulty – those few who can see them at all – by going to their images (*eikones*) and discerning the nature of that of which they are images. But Beauty, on the contrary, is bright to see, when in a happy dance the worshippers . . ., initiates in what may rightly be called the most blessed of mysteries, look on and contemplate the blessed sight. We who partake in such worship, being ourselves made perfect . . . witness in a pure light the mystery of those perfect, single, steady visions, filling us with joy. . . . (250 b)

We are told in the succeeding passage that the reason why Beauty is easier to get hold of is that its images in the world are grasped by sight, the most clear sense that we have. That is why the man whose power of 'recollection' is strong, 'the man who in heaven has looked well about him, when on earth he sees a divine-looking face, or the shape of someone's body, which is a good likeness of Beauty . . . then the efflux of Beauty comes in through his eyes, and he is put in a fever . . .' (251 a).

It is a commonplace that visual words abound in passages like these. But why should Plato find Beauty so much easier than

Righteousness or Good Behaviour ? Simply because, if what one is trying to do is to *visualise* an abstract quality, it is much easier to persuade oneself that one has succeeded in the case of Beauty than in the other cases. There goes the beautiful boy, and from him comes this 'efflux' which is associated with a sort of fever in the blood; is it not easy to imagine Plato thinking that it was possible to extract from this situation a pure image of Beauty itself, and thus be able to grasp and identify the Idea which this image resembled ? And this becomes very easy to understand, if what Plato was actually doing was treasuring a very idealised and transfigured image of the boy, forgetting about his boyishness and other irrelevant qualities, but retaining the 'efflux' and the fever in the blood. And though, as sober philosophers, we have to admit that this 'pure light' never *was* on sea or land,[1] is it not perfectly easy to understand how Plato persuaded himself that he had done the impossible ?

In the *Republic* we find him attempting something similar, but even more difficult. We can imagine him searching assiduously with his mind's eye for something which he could call 'the Righteous'; and finding it by finding its replica in large, the righteous city; to this example we shall recur shortly. And we can imagine him looking for something that he could call 'the Good', and thinking that he had described it when he had found something that was very bright, like the sun, and associated with pronounced feelings of reverence and admiration. It is because the Idea of the Good is so difficult to *visualise* that the simile or image (*eikôn*) of the sun is introduced (cf. *Rep.* 368 d, 433 a, 509 a). These conjectures have no bearing whatever on the philosophical importance of Plato's work in putting philosophy on the way to the study of the nature of universal concepts; but they may shed, perhaps, some light on what it was like to be Plato.

The same kind of difficulty is described – more prosaically than in the *Phaedrus* – in *Politicus* 285 d :

Some things (*onta* – real things, i.e. Ideas) have by nature sensible images, which are easily learnt about, and which can be indicated without difficulty, whenever anybody wants to point them out in answer to someone who is asking for an account (*logos*) of one of them; this can be done easily, with-

---

[1] Wordsworth, 'Peele Castle'.

out trouble and without saying anything (*chôris logou*). But in the case of the greatest things and the most precious there is no image (*eidôlon*) clearly wrought for men to look at, which one can show and fit to one of the senses if one wants to satisfy the mind of the questioner. That is why we have to learn by practice to be able to give an account of each thing in words, and understand it when given. For immaterial things, which are the fairest and greatest of things, can be clearly pointed out only by speech, and not by any other means.

Here we can see that Plato finds a difficulty just where, if my suggestion is right, we should expect him to find one. The things of which one can fairly easily persuade oneself that one has formed a mental image (which are the same cases as those in which, in Plato's terminology, there exists a clear *physical* image of the Idea) present no difficulty. The task for the philosopher is to do this same thing in cases where there is not this possibility. And as an aid in this task we have to use words (*logoi*).

The *logos* is, in fact, regarded by Plato as a description in words of the Idea – a description of something that is seen by the mind. The words fulfil several important functions in the enquiry. They put on record what we have seen, or claim to have seen; and to be able to give a *logos* which will stand up to questioning is the only way to substantiate such a claim. But when someone has seen an Idea, he can help someone else to see it, even if this is an Idea which has no sensible image, by means of the *logos*. There is a good example of this process in the discovery of Righteousness in the *Republic* (432 b ff.). Socrates is represented as looking at the ideal city (itself, we might say, an Idea or paradigm) and searching in it for the fourth virtue, having already discerned the other three. Do we not all, as we read this passage, picture the city to ourselves? And when Socrates finally locates what he is looking for, and gives the *logos*, do we not all direct our mind's eye to that aspect of the life of the city to which he draws our attention, namely, the fact that all the people in it are doing their own jobs? I am sure that at any rate I do; and if it be objected that this is because I have an abnormally active visual imagination, I can retort that this is a help to the understanding of Plato, who was certainly similarly endowed.

A passage that might be thought to tell against the view which I have been putting forward is *Parmenides* 130 b ff. There the young Socrates is represented as being quite happy about there being Ideas corresponding to value-words, but doubtful about some Ideas of objects which are easily imageable (man, fire and water) and still more doubtful about hair, mud (or clay) and filth, which also are imageable. But what is in question here is not, as in the passages referred to earlier, a difficulty in apprehending Ideas which are admitted to exist, but a difficulty in admitting the very existence of certain Ideas. The reason for the latter difficulty probably lies in something which is not very relevant to our present question, viz. the fact that Plato thought of the Ideas as paradigms or perfectly good examples of the classes of things of which they were Ideas. He naturally found it easier, approaching the matter in this way, to suppose that there were ideas of things which were in themselves good; possible though not so obviously necessary to admit Ideas of things which could be good or bad; and prima facie absurd to allow Ideas which would be 'perfect mud' or 'perfectly good filth' – and indeed the oddness of these expressions gives him some excuse for hesitation. But Parmenides, who speaks here with the voice of Plato, encourages Socrates to admit Ideas of any universal properties. Mud (or clay) is given in a later dialogue as a paradigm case of a *definiendum* (*Theat.* 147 a), though the word 'Idea' is not there used. In any case, whatever the explanation of the *Parmenides* passage, it has nothing to do with the difficulty or ease of forming images, and has therefore little bearing on our problem. It would constitute an objection only if I were claiming (which I am not) that Plato thought that *whenever* he was (as we should put it) having a mental image he was seeing an Idea.

VIII

The suggestion which I have been making would be put out of court if we found Plato ever talking in unambiguous terms about mental images and contrasting them with his Ideas. It will not do as counter-evidence if we find him contrasting *part* of the class of mental images with Ideas. As I have just said, I do not wish to suggest that any mental image which Plato had would have been classified by him as an Idea. There were, no doubt, plenty of mental images in his fertile imagination which he would not have called Ideas, and one of the tasks of philosophy was to separate the wheat from the chaff. I have looked for passages in which Plato is clearly talking about what we would call mental images. We can perhaps ignore as irrelevant his references to dream-images, which are fairly frequent. And we must not think that whenever the word '*phantasma*' or one of its cognates occurs, Plato is speaking of mental images. This seems to have been Aristotle's word for a mental image, though he does not always so use it (see Bonitz, *Index Aristotelicus*, s.v.); but Plato used words of this group more widely, to mean any kind of 'appearance' whether mental or perceptual. An example is *Sophist* 263-4.

I have in fact discovered two passages in which Plato is clearly talking about what we should call mental images. In neither of them does he have a *word* for 'mental image'; he borrows other words, and in one passage his language is highly metaphorical. The first passage is *Phaedo* 73 d, in which he is talking about the 'recollection' of Ideas from an earlier existence. 'Lovers,' he says, 'when they see a lyre or a coat or something else that their loved one is accustomed to use, recognise the lyre and grasp in their mind the form (*eidos*) of the boy whose lyre it is – and this is recollection.' It is significant that the words 'grasp in their mind the *eidos*' might, in another context, have been used of the intellectual grasping of an Idea. The words are not being used here in this technical sense, for the individual Cebes, for example, does not have an Idea corresponding to him. But it is not fortuitous (any more than it is in *Rep.* 510 d, to which I referred earlier) that Plato uses the word *eidos*. His point here is that, just as we can see with our minds *eidē* of individuals, so we can see with our minds the *eidos* of, for example, the Equal (as he goes on to explain).

If it be objected that it is impossible to form a mental image of the Equal, it must be admitted that in fact it is; but there is ample evidence in the text that Plato *thought* it possible. He thought, no doubt, first of two equal sticks or stones, and then of two equal non-physical lines in the mind's eye (just as we do when we are doing geometry in a naïve way), and then said 'The former have reminded me of the latter'. And the latter

he confusedly regarded as the *eidos* of Equality. This explains
how on the next page, in the course of three lines, he can
alternate so readily between the three expressions 'the equals
themselves' (plural), 'equality' (singular) and 'the equal
itself' (singular). For if one is confusedly equating the property
of being equal with a transcendent perfectly equal pair of
things, it will indeed be difficult to decide whether to use the
singular or the plural. And what easier way of getting into this
confusion than to think that to become acquainted with a
property is to do what we should call 'form a mental image of a
thing perfectly exemplifying the property' ?

To return to the previous page: the following performances
are described as being examples of the very same thing: seeing a
lyre and being reminded of its owner; seeing Simmias and being
reminded of Cebes; seeing a picture of a horse or lyre and being
reminded of a man (presumably its owner); seeing a picture of
Simmias and being reminded of Simmias (here the analogy to
being reminded of an Idea is obviously getting very close);
and lastly, seeing a pair of equal sticks or stones and being
reminded of 'the equals themselves'. There is absolutely no
suggestion in the passage of a transition from a literal to a
metaphorical sense of any of the words involved; and we may
therefore conclude that when Plato says of the last case 'seeing
equal sticks or stones or something, our mind passes from them
to that [sc. the Idea] which is different from them', the
experience to which he is referring is of just the same sort as
in the earlier cases, namely the experience which *we* should
describe as seeing with our eyes one thing, and then seeing with
our mind's eye a mental image of that thing or something else.
And so this passage, so far from affording a counter-example
to my suggestion, supports it.

IX

The other passage (*Philebus* 38–9) is not so helpful, because
in it Plato is not immediately concerned with the Theory of
Ideas. He is trying to explain the origin of, and difference
between, true and false belief. Lack of space forbids a detailed
discussion of the passage. In it, Plato is considering a case in
which a man sees an object, forms an opinion about it, and

mentally records this opinion, first in words, and then with an image of the object. The image is variously called *eikôn*, *zôgraphêma* (picture) and *phantasma ezôgraphêmenon* (appearance pictured). Plato says that both the verbal record and the pictorial one can be recalled, and that when this happens those images can be said to be true which are images 'of' true opinions and words (or propositions).

Now here Plato is clearly speaking of what we should call mental images – images, moreover, of particular objects which have been seen. It might be argued, therefore, that since Plato mentions mental images which are not Ideas, he cannot, when he speaks of Ideas, be referring to what we should call mental images. But it does not follow, from the fact that Plato sometimes mentions mental images which are not Ideas, that what he calls Ideas were not what we should call mental images. And Ideas do not in fact come in at all in this context; so it is quite possible that no relevant conclusion is to be drawn from this passage. I have tried, but failed, to find in the passage more positive evidence than this relevant to the present question. With its 'representational' model of thought, it is somewhat different from the usual Platonic approach, which regards thought as a *direct* apprehension of an object. But to discuss the difficulties raised by the passage would take us too far from our topic.

To sum up, we may say that the answer to our question which I have suggested has encountered some difficulties, but none which seems to put it altogether out of court. To this extent it remains tenable, and may have to hold the field until someone produces a more plausible answer. Or it may be that it will be shown that the question itself was illegitimate – though this would surprise me. I wish to emphasise in conclusion that I am not trying to lower Plato's reputation as a philosopher. What he did in thinking out his Theory of Ideas was of lasting importance and value for logic. We have here the beginning of the philosophical study of universals, which was the genesis of Aristotle's work in this field; and of course it very soon became apparent that mental imagery had little to do with them, and propositions (*logoi*) a great deal. Plato put his thoughts to himself, perhaps, in this unsatisfactory way because that was the way that came easiest to him, and he was (without a philosophical terminology or any but the most rudimentary philosophical tradition behind him) struggling for the first time with difficulties which would have defeated a lesser thinker. But Columbus's discovery of America is not rated any less of an achievement because he thought he was paying a visit to China.

5 Plato and the Mathematicians

In *Republic* 510 b ff., in a passage which is too well known to require quoting in full, Plato finds fault with mathematics, or at least with the mathematicians of his day. It is the purpose of this article to discuss briefly the question, What fault ? – a question which has excited a great deal of controversy among scholars, but which cannot be satisfactorily answered without broaching, as I shall do, some substantial philosophical problems.

Plato's indictment of the mathematicians rests upon two main counts: that they use physical diagrams, and that in their studies the mind 'is compelled to make its enquiry starting from *hypotheses*,[1] and proceeding not beginningwards but endwards'. Since these two grounds of attack are obscure (and are admitted by Plato to be obscure: 'I don't quite understand', says Glaucon), let us leave for the moment the question of what the *hypotheses* were, and the other question of what was wrong with using diagrams, and turn to the next thing which he says. This is, that the mathematicians 'do not, after that, think it requisite to give, either to themselves or to others, any account of these *hypotheses*, as being evident to everybody'. It is, perhaps, not so difficult to find out what Plato meant by 'give an account (*logon didonai*)' because in a later passage, in which the wording is very closely parallel, he amplifies this point (533 b ff.). There

From *New Essays on Plato and Aristotle*, ed. Renford Bambrough (Routledge and Kegan Paul, London 1964). I have, while acknowledging my own responsibility for the many errors which will surely be found in this paper, to thank Mr Richard Robinson, Professor Anders Wedberg, and Mr Renford Bambrough for their encouragement and helpful criticism. I have also to express my pleasure at finding so much to agree with in Mr Bluck's commentaries on the *Phaedo* and *Meno*, which I read after these ideas had occurred to me.

[1] I shall print this word consistently in italics, to avoid the temptation to assume that it means 'hypotheses' in any of its modern senses.

he says that mathematics 'dreams about that which is, but cannot see it with eyes awake, so long as it leaves undisturbed the *hypotheses* which it uses, and cannot give an account of them'. The 'so long as' here suggests that this defect of mathematics is remediable by undertaking the more fundamental enquiry which he calls 'dialectic'.

In the passage which follows (especially 534 b ff.) Plato says that the dialectician is the man who, unlike the mathematicians he has been attacking, 'demands, in the case of each thing, an account of its being (*logos tês ousiâs*)'; and he says, in language which echoes 510 c, that 'the man who cannot give a *logos* to himself and to another, to that extent lacks understanding (*nous*)' of the thing in question (cf. 511 d). In the immediately following and 'analogous (*hôsautôs*)' remarks about the Idea of the Good in particular, he uses the phrase 'to define by the *logos* the Idea of the Good, distinguishing it from all the other things'. Now, even if we did not know that the expression '*logos tês ousiâs*' became, for Aristotle, a technical term, which we translate 'real (or essential) definition', it would be fairly clear from these remarks that '*logon didonai*' means 'to give a definition of', in that sense of 'definition' in which to give one is to answer the question, so closely associated with Socrates, 'What is . . . ?' followed by the name of the thing under discussion. If any confirmation of this conjecture be needed, we have it in 533 b, where, instead of 'demand, in the case of each thing, a *logos* of its being', Plato gives what can only be an alternative formulation of the same point: 'demand concerning what each thing is'. There he is explicitly contrasting dialectic with mathematics.

Returning now to 510 c, we bring with us a clue to the identity of the *hypotheses* mentioned in that passage. For, whatever they are, they must be things of which (or about which) it is possible to give a *logos*; and this, we now see, means 'to say what they are'. Commentators have spent much time asking what *propositions* Plato can be referring to under the name 'hypotheses', and have suggested various more or less forced ways of interpreting the examples which he gives ('the odd and the even, and the figures, and the three kinds of angles, and other things like these') in order to extract from them propositions of some kind or another. But one cannot ask the question 'What is it?' of a proposition (e.g. the proposition that there are just three kinds of angles, or the proposition that the triangle is a three-sided rectilinear figure). Of a proposition, the appropriate question would be 'Is it true?' or 'Why is it true?' The question 'What is it?' can be appropriately asked only of a *thing*. It seems to follow that Plato means just what he says in his list of examples. Of all these things (the odd and the even, etc.), it is perfectly appropriate to ask 'What are they?'; and if we found Socrates asking such a question in one of the dialogues, we should not be in the least surprised. The reasons why it has not always been realised that the *hypotheses* here must be things, not propositions, seem to be two. The first, which is not important, is the seductive associations of the modern word 'hypothesis'. The second is that there is a very long history of 'hypothesis' meaning some kind of propositional assumption, going back to Aristotle, and, indeed, to Plato himself. In some passages in Aristotle and Plato, '*hypotheses*' are certainly propositions of some kind. But, for the reason given, it is impossible for them to be propositions here, though, as we shall see, they bring certain propositional assumptions with them.

It requires explaining how Plato can here speak of *hypotheses* as things, whereas elsewhere, and indeed perhaps elsewhere in the *Republic*, he seems to speak of them as propositions. The explanation is that in Plato the whole conception of knowledge is in a process of transition which he but dimly understood. In the *Republic* and elsewhere he frequently speaks of knowledge as if it were something analogous to sight, save that it is done not with the physical eye but with 'the eye of the mind', and that the object of this 'seeing' is not a physical object but an Idea. There has been a long transition, begun perhaps in Plato but not complete even now, from this paradigm of knowledge (knowledge, by acquaintance, of an object) to another, which might be described as 'propositional knowledge'. This is the kind of knowledge that we have when we are able truly and with certainty to *say* that something is the case. Logic cannot get very far so long as the more primitive paradigm of knowledge by acquaintance is dominant; much that is obscure in Plato becomes clearer when we realise that he is trying to give an account of logical relations between propositions on the model of quasi-physical 'connections' between things (the Ideas) which are seen with the mind's eye. What he is talking about, for example, in *Rep.* 511 b ff., is the ancestor of what we now call 'deduction'; but it is not, and cannot be, deduction as we know it, because it is conceived of, not as the discovery of a relation between propositions or even between facts, but as the quasi-physical seeing or even grasping of the quasi-visible or quasi-tangible connections between transcendental objects.

The same holds good of knowledge of any sort, including knowledge of the Ideas themselves. The Ideas are things, not propositions. The definitions of them are propositions, and it is the job of the dialectician to discover these; but the objects of knowledge (recorded in definitions) are entities (e.g. the Good) which can be 'caught hold of' (511 b) or 'looked at' (518 c and *passim*). The kind of knowledge which Plato called *noêsis* was knowledge by acquaintance of a thing, not knowledge that a certain proposition was true, though the knowledge could be expressed in a proposition or *logos* (viz. the definition of the thing). The very word which we translate 'truth' (*alêtheiâ*) means as often as not 'genuineness' (a property of a thing), and is the equivalent of '*ousiâ*' (the property of really existing) – cf. *Rep.* 524 e1 with 527 b9; and see also 525 c6.

It is not, therefore, surprising that on occasion Plato speaks of *hypotheses*, which are a kind of surrogate or second-class object of knowledge, as if they, like the objects of the best sort of knowledge, were a class of things. They are, in fact, surrogate or supposititious Ideas (at any rate in the passages we have been considering). No doubt much that is said in this – to us – primitive language could be more clearly said in the language of propositions. But we must not read too much into Plato – at least, we must not do so unguardedly, without realising that, though he was starting a great deal, he did live a very long time ago. The seeds of nearly all philosophy are to be discovered in Plato, but we must not pretend that they are more than seeds, which require the closest of scrutiny before even one who knows what they grew into can see the relation between them and it.

All this, however, does not make much clearer what, according to Plato, the mathematicians are doing, and what he thinks is wrong with it. To understand this, it may help to turn to the longest piece of mathematics that has come down to us from Plato's time, namely the well-known 'Slave' passage in the *Meno* (82 a ff.). It may be that, although it is Socrates himself who is eliciting the mathematics from the Slave, the faults which Plato mentions in the *Republic* are there exhibited. There is some indication, in the fact that the example (square and diagonal) used in the *Meno* is the same as that in *Rep.* 510 d, that Plato may have had the *Meno* passage in mind when he wrote the *Republic* passage; but it would be unwise to put any weight on this.

Socrates asks first whether the Slave speaks Greek. This is a matter of some significance (which may or may not have escaped Plato); for a rigorous geometrical demonstration depends on logic, and logic depends (in some sense, which I shall not try to make precise) on language. The geometry which is subsequently done is, as we shall see, not entirely rigorous, and depends partly upon the empirical observation of drawn figures; but even for this the Slave has to know a language – he has to be able to *recognise* the figure drawn on the sand as that to which the name 'square' can be applied.

What then happens is that Socrates draws a square and asks, 'Tell me, boy, do you know a square, that it is like this (*toiouton*) ?' The Slave says that he does. Socrates then says, 'A square figure, *therefore*, is one which has all these lines equal, being four in number ?' (my italics). The Slave agrees. But already we have had something which ought to make any geometer wince who has some regard for rigour. What is the 'therefore' doing ? How does the Slave know that the sides of a square are equal ? How, even, does he know that a square is 'like this' ? How, that is to say, does he know that the figure which Socrates has drawn *is* a square ? And what follows is as bad. Socrates goes on, 'Isn't it one, too, which has these lines across the middle equal ?' After the Slave has swallowed this, he says, 'There could be, *therefore*, a figure like this that was larger, and one that was smaller ?'

We do not need to read further; the general point has already become clear that a great deal is being *taken for granted*. A rigorous geometer who wanted to prove theorems about the square would have to include in his premises the *definition* of 'square'. In modern terms, it is because we mean by 'square', 'rhombus with equal diagonals' (or, alternatively, 'rectangle with equal sides'), and mean by these other terms what is laid down in their definitions, that we can prove the various theorems about the square. If the 'lines across the middle' are taken to be diagonals, then Socrates has at least included in his remarks the two constituents of a possible definition of 'square' ('rhombus with equal diagonals'). But even so, that a square must have these properties is being taken for granted, not shown to hold. If, as appears to be the more popular view, these lines are transversals joining the mid-points of the sides of the square, the proceeding lacks even this element of rigour.

To take another example, it is because we mean by 'circle', 'locus of a point, in a plane, equidistant from a given point' (cf. *Ep.* VII, 342 b), that we can prove the various theorems about the circle. Any of the proofs will contain a premiss to the effect that two lines are equal because they are radii of the circle; and this we know because we know, as Plato would have put it, what the Circle *is*. Socrates perhaps knew what the Square is; but there is nothing to show that the Slave did. All he does is to recognise a drawn figure as a square (most improperly, from the Platonic point of view, since no drawn figure is perfectly square), and then to agree to the general statement that squares have certain properties. This may be one reason why Socrates himself says in 85 c, at the end of the lesson, that the Slave has as yet only true belief, not knowledge; the language is like that of *Rep.* 533 b, already quoted. 'So then,' says Socrates, 'he is in a state of not knowing, and yet there are in him true beliefs about these things which he does not know ? ... And now these beliefs have been made to rise up in him like a dream. But if someone asks him these same things many times and in many ways, in the end, you may be sure, he will have as exact knowledge about them as anybody.' Here there is a hint (not the only one in the *Meno*) of what is to come in the *Republic*: to turn true belief into knowledge, dream into waking vision, the sedulous practice of dialectic is required.

But as it stands the geometry lesson in the *Meno* is open to all the strictures that Plato brings against mathematicians in the *Republic*, and helps us to understand those strictures by illustrating the faults against which they are brought. Socrates and the Slave take a figure (an example of 'the figures' mentioned as *hypotheses* in *Rep.* 510 c), 'act as if they had knowledge of it, make it their *hypothesis*' (i.e. take for granted that they have got something to talk about), 'do not after that think it requisite to give ... any *logos* of it, as being evident to everybody' (there it is, they might say, on the sand), 'but, starting from it, they now go through all the rest of their stuff and end in mutual agreement at whatever it was they set out to enquire into'. The word which I have rendered 'in mutual agreement' (*homologoumenôs*) might mean 'in agreement or consistency with their premisses'; and the same is true of the similar phrase in 533 c; but since, as we have seen, an important feature of the 'Slave' passage is that for want of rigour Socrates and the Slave make do with mutual agreement, it is tempting to take it in the former way, although it spoils an equally tempting parallel with Frege (see below).

Why is it that the Slave does not see that more is required than the bare assertion that squares have certain properties? The answer – as I have already hinted – is connected with the other criticism which Plato brings against the mathematicians in 510 d. Because he is using a visible figure which does appear to have the characteristics which are said to belong to squares, it is easy for him to assume that no further investigation is required. Socrates' initial gambit shows this: he seems to argue 'You recognise this (the drawn figure) as a square; *therefore* a square figure is one which has all these four lines equal'. There could hardly be a better illustration of the mistake that Plato is exposing in the *Republic*; a general proposition, which should be known *a priori* and by definition, is asserted merely on the basis of the empirical inspection of a single, particular, hastily drawn figure. When he wrote the *Republic*, Plato had come to think (rightly) that geometers must do better than this; and he may have been dimly aware of it even when he wrote the *Meno*.

To sum up our conclusions so far, we may say that what is wrong with the mathematicians, in Plato's view, is that they employ concepts like 'square', and assert propositions containing them, without, as a rigorous thinker must, proving these propositions on the basis of the definitions of the concepts – and that they are led to act in this way because they are using physical diagrams and taking as true what seems to be true of the diagrams. In order to sustain my thesis, it is not necessary for me to claim that definitions were never given by the mathematicians of Plato's time. There is some evidence that they sometimes were. All that is necessary for the truth of the thesis is that the essential logical role of definitions in proof should not have been realised, and that therefore mathematicians were casual about supplying and justifying them, and often omitted to do so altogether. To suppose that this was so is at least plausible, if we consider that Frege is able to make much the same complaint even about the mathematicians of a more recent time, in the well-known introduction to *Foundations of Arithmetic*. Frege was, in many ways, of a highly Platonic cast of mind, and these pages are sprinkled with passages which have (whether intentionally or unintentionally) a Platonic or Socratic ring – for example, 'The first prerequisite for learning anything is thus utterly lacking – I mean, the knowledge that we do not know.'[1] Frege begins by criticising mathematicians for employing the symbol '1' without asking what it means, or what the number one is. He protests (as Plato would have) against the identification of the number one with any of the things that are said to be 'one thing'. ' "$1 = 1$" asserts nothing of the Moon, nothing of the Sun, nothing of the Sahara, nothing of the Peak of Teneriffe; for what could be the sense of any such assertion ?'

'Questions like these', he goes on [i.e. like 'What is the number one ?'], 'catch even mathematicians for that matter, or most of them, unprepared with any satisfactory answer. Yet is it not a scandal that our science should be so unclear about the first and foremost among its objects, and one which is apparently so simple ? Small hope, then, that we shall be able to say what number is.' His own programme for putting arithmetic on a sound footing involved, above all, the defining of the key concepts in it – and rightly so, because unless we have these definitions (either explicit, or implicit by means of axioms) the science will altogether lack rigour. 'The rigour of the proof remains an illusion, however flawless the chain of deductions, so long as the definitions are justified only as an after-thought by our failing to come across any contradiction' (and still more so, he might have added, if they are not put in at all). 'By these methods we shall, at bottom, never have achieved more than an empirical certainty, and we must really face the possibility that we may still in the end encounter a contradiction which brings the whole edifice down in ruins.'[2]

On Plato's theory there is even greater need for definitions than there is on Frege's theory, because definitions had in Plato's thought an ontological as well as a logical role to play.

[1] Op. cit., trans. Austin, p. iii; cf. *Meno* 84 a–c.
[2] Op. cit., p. ix.

The kind of definition which Socrates invented, and which established itself in the systems of Plato and Aristotle, was what we call the essential or real definition – the statement, as Aristotle put it, of 'what it was, for a certain thing, to be' (or possibly 'to be what it was': e.g. of 'what it was, for a coat, to be a coat'). It was therefore natural for Plato to think that, by defining some Idea, one had proved that it existed – that by saying *what* it was, one had proved *that* it was. Aristotle saw that there was a distinction between these two things (*An. Post.* 72 a23); but Plato may have been misled by the analogy which he sometimes draws between knowing Ideas and knowing, e.g., people (cf. *Meno* 71 b). This analogy is of a piece with his tendency to treat Ideas as transcendent supremely perfect *individuals*. If one knows that a person is of a certain sort, one must (he might have argued) known, *a fortiori*, that he exists; and there is in this case justification for arguing thus, because, as Mr Strawson has recently reminded us, if we say that the King of France is wise we imply, in some sense, that he exists.[1] It is illegitimate to extend this form of argument to things like 'The Circle' (at least if we think we are establishing the existence of anything more than an *ens rationis*); if we can say what the circle is, this only establishes the possibility of speaking in a certain way, and does nothing to establish the existence of a transcendent entity called 'The Circle'. But it would have been consistent with Plato's whole outlook to think that it did establish this.

A further source of confusion may have been the following. Plato, when he wrote the *Republic*, was not clear about the distinction between the existential 'is' and the 'is' of predication. Thus, in 479 b, c, he seems not to distinguish between saying that a eunuch is not a man and saying that he (*simpliciter*, as Aristotle would have put it) is not. By the time he wrote the latter part of the *Sophist* (which may be, among other things, an attempt to grapple with this problem), Plato had perhaps become a little clearer that there was a distinction – but not so clear as Aristotle shows himself to be in *Sophistical Refutations* 167 a2. Plato may have thought, therefore, that, if I know that

---

[1] 'On Referring', *Mind* (1950); also in *Essays in Conceptual Analysis*, ed. A. G. N. Flew (1956) and in *The Theory of Meaning*, ed. G. H. R. Parkinson. The differences between Strawson and Russell are irrelevant to the present point.

the circle is the locus of a point, etc., I thereby know that the circle is, *simpliciter* (i.e. that it exists). If this conjecture is right, it would explain Plato's insistence on the three-way connection between a thing's existing, its being knowable, and the ability of the knower to give a *logos* of it (cf. *Rep.* 534 b, c, *Meno* 98 a, *Rep.* 477 a).

It remains to ask whether Plato thought that these defects in mathematics were remediable, and if so how. There is evident a certain tension in his attitude to the subject. On the one hand he describes its practitioners as 'dreaming about that which is'; on the other, he made it, in his programme of education, an absolutely obligatory 'hauling-tackle' to drag people towards reality (524 e; cf. 523 a). There are two plausible explanations. The first is that in 510 b ff. Plato is attacking the mathematicians of his day, and implying that, if they were to reform their ways, mathematics could take its place as a branch of know-ledge. 'Reform their ways' would mean, 'subject mathematics to the logical discipline of dialectic, insisting on having defini-tions of the key concepts, and on relating these definitions to that of the master-key, the Good; and thus dispensing with the visual aids on which they now rely.' The second explanation is that Plato thought that mathematics was inherently and ir-remediably defective in certain respects (viz. that it could not avoid using drawn figures, and had to get on without the support of a knowledge of the relevant Ideas), but nevertheless was valuable as a propaedeutic to the study of dialectic.

In 510 b and 511 a it is said that in mathematics the mind is 'compelled' to proceed in the way it does; and not much of a hint is given of how the practice of dialectic would improve the procedures of mathematics itself. On the other hand, it may be argued that 'compelled' means no more than 'compelled by the faulty procedures currently adopted'. In 511 c, Plato says that mathematicians, 'because they look at [the objects of their study] not by going up to a beginning, but starting from *hypotheses*, seem to you not to have understanding (*nous*) about them, although they are intelligible (*noēta*) if linked with a beginning'. The meaning of the last phrase is disputed; but one possible interpretation of it is that, once mathematics is 'connected up' by dialectic with the Idea of the Good, it becomes a branch of knowledge proper. This is supported by 533 c:

G

'it cannot see with eyes awake, *so long as* it leaves undisturbed the *hypotheses* which it uses'. This seems to imply that once the *hypotheses* are 'disturbed', dream may yield to reality. And in the *Meno* passage, as we saw, it is said that the true opinion which the Slave has is capable of being turned into knowledge by a longer course of questioning (85 c).

We may perhaps take it, then, that the first of the defects of mathematics, that which consists in its wrong use of *hypotheses*, is ultimately remediable, though no doubt inescapable in the initial stages of instruction. What of the second defect – the use of figures ? If to give up the use of figures in geometry would be to do analytical geometry, expressed by means of algebraical symbols alone, then it would be anachronistic to suppose that Plato had any such thing in mind – although the line of thought which he was starting, with its insistence on logical as opposed to empirical proofs, led ultimately to this conclusion. But we must not be confused here by an assumption which commentators have been too ready to make, namely, that among the figures that Plato wished to reject are to be included not only figures drawn on the sand, but also figures looked at with the mind's eye – i.e. what we should call, though Plato would not have, 'imagined figures'. There is no indication in the text that Plato frowned on the use of the latter. Indeed, there is some evidence that he thought of looking at things with the mind's eye as a paradigm of true knowledge,[1] and as what ought to take the place of looking at physical things (e.g. drawn figures) with the physical eye, when empirical observation gave way to logical thought. If this view is correct, then Plato may have considered that the empirical procedures of current mathematics could be superseded, without having thought of anything so advanced as analytical geometry.

We may, then, hazard a guess that Plato thought both the defects of contemporary mathematics remediable ultimately by the help of dialectic, though unavoidable in the schoolroom. But how did he think that dialectic could help ? To ask this is to raise a very large question, about which, since it is still very obscure to me, I can only make some tentative suggestions. The remarks which I have made about the mathematicians' *hypotheses* and their use of them are not intended to apply to

[1] See the preceding essay.

the dialecticians' use of the same (or it may be different) *hypotheses*. It may be that these latter, unlike the *hypotheses* mentioned in 510 c, *are* some kind of *logoi* or propositions – though there are difficulties in this view, and I have found no strong support for it in the text of this passage. In the *Phaedo*, likewise, it may be that the *hypotheses* referred to are *logoi* (though Mr Bluck seems to argue against this view; see his *Phaedo*, p. 165). In the *Meno*, where *hypotheses* are said to be used by mathematicians and where one is used by Socrates in his argument, they seem to be propositions, as even Mr Bluck evidently agrees – but, lest this should be taken as casting doubt on what I have said about the mathematicians' use of *hypotheses* in the *Republic*, it must be pointed out that it is hard to find much similarity between what the mathematicians are said to be doing with their *hypotheses* in the *Meno*, and what they are said to be doing with them in the *Republic*, or even between the *hypotheses* themselves (*Meno*, 86 e ff.).

What is the dialectician supposed to be achieving, and how is this going to help the mathematician? We have already seen that it is the aim of the dialectician to establish definitions. If this is so, his task is a good deal easier than it would be on some other views about what he is trying to do. It is not possible to explain why, without a short excursus into the relations between logic and metaphysics. Metaphysics, or much of it, is logic in ontological dress; it is logic done in the material mode of speech. For example, when Socrates asks 'What is mud (or clay) ?' and gives the answer 'Earth mixed with water' (*Theaet.* 147 a), the status of both the question and the answer is equivocal. There is no doubt that Plato and Aristotle would have regarded the definitions which are the answers to such questions as synthetic statements about the natures or essences of the *definienda*, which for Plato were Ideas. Yet they are also thought of as having the *a priori* character which belongs to definitions in most modern senses of the word. That is to say, once we realise that mud *is* earth mixed with water, we are supposed to know this as a necessary truth about mud. In short, the Socratic-Platonic-Aristotelian essential definition, the archetype of all synthetic *a priori* propositions, tries to have it both ways. It tries both to be a synthetic statement about an existing thing (in Plato's case, an Idea), and to have the necessity of a definition (or, to be more accurate, of something that is true by definition.)

It would be out of place to argue here the question whether there can be any such synthetic *a priori* truths; for our historical purpose it is enough to assume that Plato thought that there could, and to ask how it made the dialectician's task seem easier to him than it might to a modern.

Those who believe in the possibility of synthetic *a priori* truths are accustomed, when it comes to discovering or proving them, to lean heavily on their *a priori* character. That is to say, they use arguments which, although they are supposed to prove something synthetic, in fact consist covertly or overtly in appeals to language and meaning. Thus, if anybody denied that mud was earth mixed with water, it might be said that if anything were earth mixed with water it must be mud, and vice versa – and this would be said with the implication that anybody who doubted it just couldn't be understanding the words.[1] Now if it were avowed that what was being asserted was that 'mud' *meant* 'earth mixed with water' (if, that is to say, the synthetic character of the conclusion to be established were given up), this would be a perfectly legitimate argument. I want to maintain that Plato's suggested procedure is covertly linguistic in character, though he himself did not understand this.

Let us take as an example the definition of the Circle. Suppose that a dialectician has this word '*kyklos*' (meaning as much 'wheel' as 'circle'), which is in common use, and asks himself the question 'What, really, *is* the *kyklos*?' Now no doubt Plato thought that the dialectician would be asking this question about a real object of thought transcending this world, and that the answer would be a synthetic statement; but, nevertheless, in arriving at and testing such a definition by dialectical methods he would be, unwittingly perhaps, appealing to the ordinary use of the word, or a tidied-up version of it. He would propound suggested definitions, and see whether, when the word was used in the way suggested, it led to absurdities – i.e. to things that, since words mean what they do, nobody would

[1] We may ignore, as irrelevant to our present problem, another possible interpretation of the statement 'Mud is earth mixed with water': viz. as meaning 'If one takes a certain recognisable substance called earth and mixes it with another called water, the result will always be some stuff of the sort called mud; and this is the only way of producing this stuff.' So interpreted, it is an empirical proposition. It is confusion with this quite different proposition that enables the definition to masquerade as synthetic.

be willing to say. If this were what the dialectician was doing, he would be following a method in philosophy which seems a good one and still has many adherents.[1] And this view is supported by the fact that the definitions which Plato gives us (e.g. 'Mud is earth mixed with water' and 'The circle is the locus of a point equidistant, etc.' – to say nothing of those in the Academic dictionary called *Definitions*, many of which no doubt go back to him) are such as would very naturally and properly be established by such a method. It seems to be this kind of procedure that is being referred to in *Rep.* 534 b ff., and we see it actually in operation in *Rep.* 331 c and elsewhere.

It has often been objected to such a method (substantially similar to the Socratic elenchus) that, relying as it does on the mere failure to refute a proposed view, it does nothing to establish its truth; for it is one thing to fail to show that a view is false, and another to show positively that it is true. When what we are trying to establish are definitions, however, it is not clear that this objection is well taken. It is not even clear that it is a fair one in some other fields; scientists, according to Professor Popper,[2] never prove their hypotheses but only fail, after trying hard, to falsify them. This analogy with scientific method may show (however reluctant Plato would have been to admit it) that there is after all an empirical element in the elenchus; are we not, in practising it, looking for possible falsifications of the empirical hypothesis that, in their ordinary discourse, people use a word in a certain way? This problem is still a very obscure one; and it may be that Plato could answer this last objection (see my article just referred to).

If a group of people, who know the language in which the word 'circle' occurs, are trying to find out 'its meaning', they may think that they have done so with sufficient certainty when they have discovered a definition which accords with their own use of the word, and which, try as they may, co-operatively and dialectically – i.e. by trying out the definition in actual discourse – they cannot fault by showing that it leads to absurdity, or to saying things which, as they do use the word, one cannot say. It would perhaps not be unreasonable for such a group of people, if they were untutored enough to use the material mode of speech, to say that they had discovered for

[1] I have discussed it, and some of the difficulties in it, in the second essay in this volume.   [2] *The Logic of Scientific Discovery* (1956) esp. pp. 32 ff.

certain what a circle *was*. Even now, when linguistic philosophers have been arguing for a long time about some point of
usage (for example, the question 'Can I say "I intend to do A,
although I am certain that I shall not succeed in doing it" ?'),
they seem, sometimes, to satisfy themselves, justifiably or not,
that they know what the right answer is. Perhaps, therefore,
it was pardonable, even if in the end incorrect, for Plato to think
that one could, by the method he alludes to, achieve certainty
that evening *is* the ending of the day, or that wind *is* the movement of air around the earth (*Def.* 411 b, c). And he may have
thought that the same method was applicable to more difficult
terms (including those of mathematics); here the going would
be harder, but there are some gallant attempts in the *Definitions*
and scattered throughout the canonical works of Plato. After
all, he never claims that dialectic is easy.

One further factor (already noticed) may have made the
goal of dialectic seem to Plato possible of attainment. He thought
that knowledge was, like sight, some kind of apprehension of an
object, but with the mind's eye. If, therefore, the dialectician
was not merely submitting his *logoi* to the elenchus, but all the
time searching with his mind's eye for the thing he was trying
to define – as were all the participants in the discussion – and
scrutinising carefully all the possible candidates, it was perhaps
doubly easy for him to think that in the end they would all fix
their mental eyes on the same thing, be satisfied of its genuineness, and be able to produce an indestructible definition of it.
It was natural for him to conclude that, in that case, they would
have achieved knowledge – especially since, in his view, they
had already, in a previous existence, had knowledge of the
thing and had only to recollect it.

However, we have not yet exhausted the answers to objections
that Plato might have thought available to him. For he evidently
thought that the pieces of knowledge, so acquired, were related
to each other in some sort of system, and could therefore re-
inforce one another; and in particular he thought that all the
other objects of knowledge (Ideas) were in some way 'attached'
to the Idea of the Good (511 b). We have now to ask how this
helped, and in particular what was the relevance of the Idea
of the Good to mathematics.

The following reflections may help us to understand Plato's

thought. If we try to draw a circle, somebody may say 'That isn't a very good circle'. By this he might be taken to mean that it is not very exactly circular – that it is not the sort of circle that one would point to if one wished to give somebody an idea of what a circle was. Here 'good' seems to be being used in such a way that the criteria for being a good circle are identical with those for being (really) a circle. This use of the word (meaning roughly, 'good specimen of') is, it is hardly necessary to point out, to be distinguished from other uses more relevant to moral philosophy. There is a long line of philosophers, stretching from Plato through Aristotle and Aquinas to Mr Geach, who have, through confusion on this point, thought that we could find out what it was to be a good man by finding out what it was to be a man.[1] Plato did not in general distinguish this use of 'good' from others; indeed, he perhaps thought that this use could, by analogy, illuminate the others. And since there was, for him, a single Idea of the Good, it was natural for him to suppose that knowledge of this Idea would put him in a position to tell good circles from bad circles, good men from bad men . . . and, in short, a good anything from a bad anything. And to know what it was to be a good ϕ would be to know what it was to be, really, a ϕ. This is implicit in his view that the Idea of anything was (perhaps among other things) the paradigm or perfectly good specimen of that kind of thing.[2]

So Plato may have argued as follows. If we wish to know what it is to be a circle (to know the Idea of circularity, or to know what the Circle is), we have to find out what it is to be a good or perfect circle. And this involves knowing the Idea of the Good, or what the Good is. Thus knowledge of the Idea of the Good is necessary to complete our knowledge of all the other Ideas. Since to be (really) a circle, a figure has to be a good circle, the Good can be said to be the source of the being and the reality of the circle – and of everything else likewise (cf. 509 b and, perhaps, *Phaedo* 97 e ff.). This would sufficiently explain why Plato thought the study of the Good to be the coping-stone of the mathematical sciences (534 e).

[1] See Geach's article and my reply in *Analysis* (1956–7) (reprinted in *Theories of Ethics*, ed. P. Foot).

[2] See G. Vlastos, *Philosophical Review*, LXIII (1954) (reprinted in *Studies in Plato's Metaphysics*, ed. R. E. Allen).

Unfortunately for Plato, this line of thought is fallacious. As Aristotle saw (*Eth. Nic.* 1 6), there is no *single* quality of goodness which is possessed by all good things, and to know which would be to know what made them all good, and thus (if the confusion just mentioned be swallowed) to know what made them the things that they are. What makes a circle a good circle is *different* from what makes a square a good square or a man a good man. Aristotle's view seems to have been that the word 'good' *meant* something different in these different contexts; and in this he may have been wrong. But he was right in thinking that the *criteria* of goodness were different for different kinds of things; and this is fatal to Plato's programme. For if there is no common quality of goodness common to all good things, to know what makes two different kinds of thing good is to have two different pieces of knowledge.[1]

It might be thought that a closer understanding of the difference between the meaning of the word 'good' and the criteria for its application to different things might vitiate Aristotle's attack, and so save Plato. But this is not so. It is true that Aristotle has not demonstrated that 'good' does not have a common *meaning*, but only that there are not common criteria for its application. And so we may allow Plato the premiss that 'good' always means the same, of whatever class of objects it is used (subject to the qualification made above, that sometimes the words 'specimen of' need to be supplied). But this premiss is gained only by divorcing meaning from criteria; and so, although it may be the case that by knowing one thing – namely, what 'good' means – we shall know what it means whatever word it precedes, this will not now do for us what Plato thought it would. For to know what 'good' in 'good circle' means will not now help us to know what makes a circle a good circle. For that, we shall have to find out two more things, viz. what a circle is, and what are the qualities which make a circle a good one. And though in this particular case (because 'specimen of' is understood), these two questions may come to the same thing, there will be the further difficulty that in other cases (e.g. that of 'man') they are quite different questions.

Nevertheless, it is easy to suppose that, when he wrote the

[1] Cf. Aristotle, *Eth. Nic.* 1096 a29 ff., and my *Language of Morals*, pp. 99 ff.

Republic, these difficulties had not occurred to Plato. For one of the impressions which it is hard to avoid when reading these pages is that he had not, when he wrote them, carried out in detail the programme of enquiry which he is proposing. When he did, he encountered difficulties; and that is why the account of dialectic given in later dialogues is different in many respects. Aristotle also, in trying to carry on with the Platonic programme, met with further obstacles, and his methodology becomes different again, though still related in obvious ways to Plato's. In the *Republic* we have little more than a tantalising prospectus.

If this is a defect, this article must share it; for I have not had time to undertake the detailed study which would be necessary to turn the suggestions which I have made into more than suggestions. Much remains to be discovered; and my only excuses for putting these ideas into print are, first, that I could not resist a tempting invitation, and secondly, that the work which I hope to do on this subject will be greatly assisted by such criticisms as this article may receive.

6 The Practical Relevance of Philosophy

As I set out to argue that philosophy can have a practical relevance, I can hardly begin better than by pointing to that distinguished philosopher, who is at the same time the most practical of men, my predecessor in the White's chair. William Kneale is a paradigm of practical philosophy, not only because he is a man to whom one naturally turns for help on any practical question – as the University did about the possibilities of changes in its curriculum – but for a more significant reason. Although he added distinction to this chair of moral philosophy, and has done important work in that field, his interests do not lie primarily there; but like his own great predecessor John Austin, his work in other fields of philosophy is of importance for all branches of the subject – of such importance that no moral philosopher can afford to neglect it. For philosophy is a unity; and if the bearing of philosophy on practice comes – as it does – chiefly through moral philosophy, nevertheless the other work of philosophers shares in this practical relevance, in that nobody could be a competent moral philosopher who did not spend as much time on it as on his own speciality. In retiring from Oxford to Yorkshire, I am sure that the Kneales, both of them, have not deserted philosophy, and that we may expect their retirement to be as fruitful as we wish it happy. Indeed, we are to have the first-fruits of it in ten days' time, his Marett Lecture.

It is very important to be clear that philosophy has a practical relevance; I for one should not be studying it unless I thought it had. Academic disciplines can be divided, as Plato divided goods in book II of the *Republic*, into those which are good in themselves, those which are useful for some ulterior purpose, and those which are both. Philosophy falls, as Plato thought

Inaugural Lecture delivered at Oxford, 1967.

righteousness fell, into the third and best class of goods. If it fell only into the first – if it were worth pursuing only for the mere pursuit's sake – then it would indeed deserve a place in our syllabus; but it would perhaps not be able to claim a very large share in our limited resources. I shall in this lecture, while allowing that the pursuit of philosophy is a good in itself – it has, at least, an entertainment-value as high as that of some less utilitarian studies – maintain that it is also a useful vocation. I shall be speaking primarily of moral philosophy; if this has a use, then the other parts of philosophy also have a use, because they are indispensable to it; this does not mean that they have not also independent uses of their own.

I shall start by surveying the field upon which moral philosophy might be expected to have a bearing, namely, the field of practical moral problems, and ask whether in fact moral problems exist such as really do trouble us. This might seem hardly necessary, were it not for the considerable number of people one meets in a sophisticated place like Oxford who deny that they ever think about moral problems or make moral judgements, and the even larger number of people in less sophisticated places who seem to be acting in accordance with a similar policy. After that I shall examine the main theoretical argument against the practical relevance of moral philosophy. I hope to show that, though this argument is a justified protest against certain illegitimate ways of seeking to make it relevant, and against certain misconceptions of the nature of morality, it leaves untouched the real bearing of philosophy on practice. I hope to end by demonstrating this bearing in the only convincing way, by actually saying something important, as a philosopher, about a practical question.

Are there nowadays any moral problems that trouble people ? Certainly, to anyone who does not lead too cloistered a life, or even anyone who reads the newspapers, it must be obvious that there are many more than can be even listed in a lecture. In the field of legislation, we have recently had two important bills debated, one about homosexuality and the other about abortion. The arguments put forward on both sides in the debates on those bills are in the main moral arguments. For example, the question of whether a doctor ought to be allowed to terminate a pregnancy when it is highly probable that the child will be born seriously deformed is a moral problem.

Perhaps the sophisticated people I have mentioned do not feel themselves called on to have views on such questions; or perhaps they do not read the newspapers. But those who do, and who look around them, know what an enormous amount of human misery or happiness depends on what answers legislators give to them. Doctors and legislators would have a just cause of complaint against philosophers if, being in a position to shed light on these problems, they failed to do so. When, recently, together with some other philosophers, I sat on a committee which was discussing abortion, I felt that moral philosophy was an essential piece of equipment for understanding the problem and deciding what ought to be done. And I could say the same about many other moral problems which have troubled me personally.

In the field of international affairs, likewise, acute moral problems continually arise. At the time of the Suez fiasco, some normally very enlightened people were going round asking their colleagues to sign a declaration which said, among other things, that the Government's action in invading Egypt was morally wrong. I signed the document, and I am sure that I was right to do so, although the reasons given for saying that the action was morally wrong were almost as absurd as those given for saying that it was morally right. At the present time, at least part of the debate that is going on about what ought to be done in Vietnam is a debate about moral questions. If the questions were not moral, they would be a good deal easier to answer, though still far from easy.

In the same way, if we take almost at random any field of domestic policy – say that concerning education – another crop of moral problems arises. There is, for example, the question of equality in education: is it right to devote equal resources to the education of each child, irrespective of ability; or ought we, as some advocate, to devote more resources to educating abler children; or, as others urge, devote more resources to educating less able children, in order to compensate for their handicap ? Arguments of a moral sort could be adduced for each of these three courses; but I shall not pursue them. Then there are all the questions about moral education itself: to what extent is it legitimate for one generation to try to influence the moral attitudes of the next generation, and by what means ? What is the difference between moral education, which most of us applaud, and indoctrination, which most of us condemn ? What is a morally educated man ? What, in general, ought parents, teachers and others to be trying to do to the young ?

There is no reason why I should stop this list of moral questions, except that I have now to go on to say what I think the philosopher can contribute to their solution. Some of you will have heard me discussing one or two of these problems in some detail in my ordinary lectures. Here I have to be more general. Let us next, therefore, examine the argument which has led some philosophers to think that they can contribute little. The argument rests on three premises. I shall not dispute the truth of these premises. In fact, I agree with them – though all of them require rather more careful formulation than I shall be able to give them in this very summary lecture. I will go further and say that all three are not merely true, but of fundamental importance. The first premiss is a thesis about the scope and nature of philosophy. In its essence it goes back to Socrates. Socrates, we may say, started philosophy as we know it by refusing to answer questions of substance like 'Is it right and proper to prosecute my father when he has unintentionally killed a slave of his ?' before he had been given an answer to conceptual questions about the meanings of the crucial terms in them, such as 'right' and 'proper'. From that day to this, most philosophers have recognised these conceptual questions as being central to philosophy. They have, no doubt, differed about what one is doing when one elucidates a concept. Is one, as Plato thought, trying to discern the nature of a subsistent transcendental entity whose name is the word in question ? Or is one rather, as other philosophers have thought, trying to define or analyse a word ? I shall not discuss this controversy, because it is irrelevant to the matter in hand. Actually, I think that, when we fully understand the point at issue, we see that there is *no* point at issue; there really is no difference between trying to discern the nature of the thing called 'right' and trying to define or analyse the word 'right'. The philosophical task can be described in either way, and, however described, is to be distinguished (as Socrates distinguished it) from the task of deciding what it is right and proper to do. Socrates, besides distinguishing the tasks, thought, unlike many moderns, that one was an important preliminary to the other; and I agree with him.

The elucidation of concepts, which, as I have said, was always central to the activity of the philosopher, has been at various times surrounded by other activities, also included under the name 'philosophy'. In this university, in which the Sedleian Professor of Natural Philosophy and Dr Lee's Professor of Experimental Philosophy still bear those titles, although working within the Faculty of Physical Sciences, I do not need to emphasise this point. With increasing specialisation, and with increasing clarity about the distinctness of different methods, these activities have become separated from what is usually called philosophy; and thus it has come to be confined to what, as I have said, was always its central core. Of course, the same person may do more than one thing, even in the course of a single work (as, for example, Whitehead did some philosophy and some mathematics); nor is it always easy to tell which a man is doing at any one moment, just as it is not easy to tell whether, say, Einstein is at a particular time doing mathematics or physics – or for that matter philosophy. However, this does not destroy the distinction between mathematics and physics, or between either and philosophy. The distinction is between different methods, and the question is one of what can be accomplished by these different methods – the words do not matter.

When, therefore, in this lecture I speak of 'philosophy', I want you to understand me as referring to its central core, the elucidation of concepts. Somebody who used the term more widely would have no difficulty in showing the relevance of philosophy to all manner of questions. If, for example, we were to use it in the wide sense in which we can speak, as some people do speak, of 'the philosophy of dry-fly fishing' (meaning 'the general principles of dry-fly fishing'), then there would be no difficulty in showing the relevance of philosophy to dry-fly fishing. But I have set myself a harder task than this.

The second premiss in the argument is that the elucidation of concepts can never by itself yield synthetic conclusions about matters of substance. Just as, nowadays, no scientist tries, by metaphysical, conceptual reasonings alone, without empirical data, to arrive at conclusions of substance about how the world works, so, in moral philosophy, it is widely, and ought to be universally, recognised that you cannot establish moral principles of substance by elucidating the meanings of words – not just by that.

From these two premises it would seem to follow that, if we are, by means of philosophical reasoning, to arrive at conclusions of substance about how we ought to act, we need to put into the reasoning, somewhere, synthetic, substantial premises of some sort. The only possible dispute seems to be about what these premises can be. Undoubtedly the most popular way of trying to bring philosophy to bear on practical questions, while admitting the truth of the two premises I have just mentioned, is to say that the required synthetic premises can be empirical ones. If it were possible to start from empirical premises, established by ordinary observation and the familiar procedures for predicting the future, and from them, by the conceptual transformations which philosophy discovered, get to substantial moral conclusions, then philosophy would really have done something for the solution of practical problems. This is the programme of the kind of moral philosophy usually called 'naturalism'. And throughout history a very large part of our profession has been occupied in the search after this philosopher's stone for turning empirical propositions into moral judgements. In its essence the programme of naturalism is this: we have, in elucidating the moral concepts, to give such an account of them as will make it possible to deduce moral judgements of substance from non-moral, factual premises.

I have already given in so many places my reasons for rejecting this programme as impossible of fulfilment that I will not bore you by giving them again. Instead, I shall merely record my own acceptance of the third premiss on which the argument against the practical relevance of philosophy has been based. This premiss is the rejection of naturalism. It does not terribly matter for our purposes how it is formulated; but it comes to this, that, the moral concepts being what they are, no account of them could in principle be given which would enable one to pass by a logical deduction from empirical or other factual premises to a moral conclusion.

The argument against the practical relevance of philosophy is based, then, on these three premises: first, philosophy is concerned centrally and essentially with the elucidation of concepts; secondly, from such elucidation, by itself, no substantial or synthetic conclusion of any kind can follow; and thirdly, the elucidation will never give us a means of deducing moral judgements from statements of fact. I think that a great many moral philosophers have been impelled to attack one or other of these premises, or the distinctions on which they rely, just because they wanted to justify philosophy as a practically relevant discipline, and could see no way of doing so except by challenging the premises on which the argument is based. Thus it has seemed important to some philosophers to claim that philosophy is more than the elucidation of concepts – that it can yield knowledge of a realm of non-empirical being which is at the same time a source of values; or that the elucidation of concepts can lead us to synthetic conclusions; or that it is possible to find a way by conceptual analysis from facts to moral judgements. To others it has seemed best to deny the possibility of distinguishing, as the argument requires, between analytic and synthetic propositions, or between descriptive and evaluative judgements – two distinctions which are so closely related that it is hardly possible to maintain the second while rejecting the first. These claims have often been made by the same people, and they have, I think, often had the same motive, which was to defend philosophy against the imputation of practical irrelevance. Others have accepted the argument and admitted the charge, justifying the practice of philosophy solely for its own intrinsic interest.

I do not myself agree with any of these positions; but I shall not now criticise them, since it would take a lecture apiece to do so with any pretence of adequacy. I propose to argue for the practical relevance of philosophy in a different way; accepting the three premises, I shall challenge the cogency of the argument that is based on them. I want to maintain that the argument has seemed cogent only because of a radical misconception about the nature of moral reasoning. If moral reasoning were the sort of thing that it has usually been thought to be, then, given the three premises, it would really be impossible for philosophers, or for that matter anybody else, to discover a rational method of solving practical moral problems. If I may caricature this view about moral reasoning, it is something like this: the only way to reach a moral conclusion is to have some premises which cannot be doubted, and proceed by some approved and certified method of inference from them to a moral conclusion. I wish you to note that what is wrong with this scheme is not the insistence on certitude in the premises or in the mode of inference; a method of reasoning which sought to get from probable premises to probable conclusions by means of reasonably reliable modes of inference would be open to the same objection. What is wrong with this kind of reasoning is what we may call, borrowing and slightly altering in sense a term of Bosanquet's, its linearity. It is supposed to start from something given, and proceed in a straight line – or at any rate a line – until it arrives at the conclusion.

Now, as has often been pointed out, scientists do not proceed in this way, and I can see no reason why moralists should. It is an entirely inappropriate method for any discipline which seeks synthetic conclusions. But if you think that this is the only way in which moral reasoning can proceed, you are going to be in trouble, given the three premisses which we have granted. For what are going to be the undoubted or probable starting-points of the reasoning ? Because of the second premiss, they cannot be the conceptual or analytic findings of philosophy, which, because of the first premiss, are all the philosopher can supply. Because of the third premiss, they cannot consist solely of matters of fact supplied by the empirical sciences or by ordinary observation and prediction. Nor, for more complicated but essentially similar reasons, can they consist of any combination of these elements. So there is nothing that the reasoning could be founded on that could, in principle, be the grounds for a moral conclusion.

I should like you to notice that I have said nothing as yet about the so-called prescriptivity of moral judgements. This is not required as a premiss in setting up the argument which is thought to show the practical irrelevance of moral philosophy. It is true that the prescriptivity of moral judgements is in fact the reason for the truth of the third premiss (that which forbids 'is' – 'ought' deductions of substance). But this premiss has nevertheless been maintained by philosophers who were not prescriptivists; and although prescriptivism, once accepted, provides some good arguments in support of the premiss, the most famous arguments for it do not depend on any thesis about the prescriptivity of moral judgements. I shall introduce prescriptivity into this lecture, not to buttress these arguments, but in order to show the way out of the difficulty, as you will see.

Though linear inferences can occur in moral reasoning, as they can also occur in scientific reasoning, they cannot (however essential) be its only or its most important method. This is

H

the first clue to the solution of our problem; and the second is that moral reasoning has to involve the will (which is an old-fashioned way of saying that moral judgements, or the most important and typical part of them, are prescriptive; and that this fact places a restriction on the kinds of reasoning that could possibly have a moral conclusion: it has to be the kind of reasoning in which and by which we come to prescribe something). I want now to clear away a common misconception about the view which I have just adumbrated. In what follows I am certainly not going to say that *factual statements about* what people will or want or prescribe can supply the missing ingredient in our moral reasoning, which will enable us to reach moral conclusions by a form of argument revealed by philosophers. To say this would be to invite obvious objections. We should still be trying to get moral conclusions from factual premisses, which is forbidden by the third premiss which I accepted – namely, from factual premisses about what people want, etc. It would also incur the charge of subjectivism; we should be deriving moral conclusions from the fact that somebody had a certain subjective attitude; and against such a procedure there are well-known objections which I shall not rehearse. Not that my own view is a form of objectivism either; in so far as the terms 'objectivism' and 'subjectivism' still have a use in moral philosophy, they refer to two equally mistaken views, which, indeed, share a common defect – namely the assimilation of moral judgements to purely descriptive, factual statements. If moral judgements were purely factual or descriptive, it would be possible to ask whether the facts they stated were subjective facts about the speaker, or objective facts about whatever he was describing. But if they are not purely factual – if there is an element in their meaning which is not descriptive – it makes no sense to ask, of this element, whether it conveys something objective or subjective. What it conveys is something that could not be either objective or subjective.

There is, however, an even more important objection to the view that moral reasoning is founded upon statements of fact about what people will or want or prescribe. One of the most essential features of moral reasoning is that, in the course of it, and because of it, our desires, or what we will, can *change*; facts about a man's desires cannot, therefore, be used as a fixed datum from which he reasons to a moral conclusion.

However, it is easy to confuse this mistaken proposal with that which I shall be making, and so I would ask you to be attentive to the difference. We find ourselves, and we find other people, with certain desires; this is where we start. So far there is no difference between my view and the mistaken, subjectivist view I have just mentioned. These desires, if expressed, would be expressed in the form not of statements (this is the first difference), but of prescriptions – of *singular* prescriptions of the form 'Let me do *x*' or 'Let me have *y* done to me'. But (and this is the second difference) we do not *reason from* these desires or these prescriptions; we *operate upon* them by subjecting them to a certain requirement: the requirement that what we desire or prescribe for ourselves, we have to desire or prescribe for anyone else in like situations. Our singular prescriptions have to be, as it has been put, 'universalised'. When faced with this requirement – a requirement laid upon us by the nature or meaning of the moral concepts – we shall abandon some of our desires. They will not go through this sieve. By this I do not mean that we shall necessarily abandon them *qua* desires – we may still go on *wanting* to have the only remaining drink of water in this part of the desert; but we shall not be able to think that we *ought* to take it (we shall not be able to accept this implicitly *universal* prescription for *anyone* in our position) because we cannot desire or prescribe that anyone else should take it at the cost of ourselves going thirsty. The *appetites* may remain unchanged by the exercise of reason; but if we are, in Kantian terms, seeking to will something as a universal law, or, as Aristotle put it, willing and acting in accordance with a principle (*kata logon tâs orexeis poioumenoi kai prâttontes*),[1] we shall subordinate these appetites to the rational will. And if we are reasoning morally – if we are seeking an answer to the question 'What *ought* I to do?' – that is a discipline to which we have to submit. It is a discipline laid upon us, analytically, by the meaning of the word 'ought', which is to be discovered by a purely conceptual enquiry. This much philosophy can contribute.

I have said that when faced with the requirement to universalise, we shall abandon some of our desires, or subordinate them to the rational will. Shall we thus, inevitably, be led, as Kant seems to have thought, to a single unique system of moral principles? I do not think so; what I think will be achieved is

[1] *Eth. Nic.* 1095 a10.

something more modest. In matters in which no conflicts of interest arise between people, I can see this method leading to very different sets of principles. In matters where interests do conflict, which form the greater part of the moral problems that most trouble us, I think that all but a very few people, if any at all, will be led to moral principles which resemble, with relatively minor variations, those which are commonly accepted in most societies. The reason for this is that, in order to diverge from this norm, in matters in which conflicts of interest arise, one would have to be not only a person with very extraordinary desires, but one who was prepared to stick to these desires at the cost of the abnegation of desires which for nearly everybody are among their strongest. An example would be a person who has the most intense desire to torture people for his own enjoy-ment, and is not prepared to subordinate this desire to any others; he is prepared to accept and indeed welcome a principle which allows him to do this, even if it also allows other people, correspondingly, to torture him for *their* enjoyment in similar circumstances, were such circumstances to occur. And remember that the circumstances would have to be similar in this respect also, that he would have as strong a desire not to be tortured as his victim now has. For this reason an ordinary masochist would not do as an example of the sort of person we are looking for.

The practical value of the method of reasoning I have sketched is enhanced if such people are, as I think they are, extremely rare; but it does not rest entirely on such a supposition; for it may, I think, be at least assumed that in a *great many* of the moral problems which trouble us, *most* people will be brought by this method, if once they understand the moral concepts well enough to grasp it, to agree with one another in their universalised prescriptions or desires or wills; and we shall then have a basis for moral agreement, and for these people (that is to say nearly all of us) the moral problems will have been solved.

I could, if I had time, illustrate the practical utility of the method I have outlined by applying it to some particular moral problem that vexes us. I have done this elsewhere; but in what remains of this lecture I am going to ask a different sort of practical question, on which also these theoretical remarks have a bearing. If the nature of morality is as I have described it, how does that affect its future? Indeed, has it a future?

Nobody who looks about him and listens and reads a little can fail to be struck by the prevalence, nowadays, of an attitude to which I have already referred, and which I am going to call 'amoralism'. This attitude is, as I said, not confined to intellectuals, but permeates our society. Or perhaps, when I say that amoralism permeates our society, I am taking things too much at their face value. Perhaps what permeates our society is not strictly speaking amoralism. It is something more complicated. Amoralism is a refusal to make moral judgements or ask moral questions. But what, I think, permeates our society is rather a pose of amoralism which can be assumed only by those who either misconceive the nature of morality, or do not think very clearly, or do not get too deeply involved in life. Scratch an amoralist of this spurious sort, or on the other hand get him to think clearly about some matter which concerns him closely, and he will start to moralise, though he may not call it that. The real amoralist, like the man who is really prepared to universalise his desire to torture people for his own enjoyment, is such a rarity that he need not claim much of the attention of people whose concern for the future of morality is a practical one.

What makes people into amoralists of this spurious sort? I think that the most important factor is a misunderstanding of what morality is. I have given my own account of what it is; but what the 'amoralist' is rejecting is not the sort of thing that I have been describing. That is why I say that he misconceives the nature of morality. There are a lot of rules which have come down to us which we do indeed, in a sense, call moral rules or principles, and which say that we ought, or (more commonly) ought not, to do this or that. These rules, which are what the amoralist means by morality, are of a highly general sort; they characterise the kinds of action which we ought to do or abstain from in very simple ways, without exceptions or qualifications. Those who admire these principles, and insist that we should have them, often seem to make it a requirement that to count as a moral principle a principle should not be merely universal in the logical sense (for of course even a very complicated and specific principle could be universal in that sense, provided that it made no essential reference to individuals), but should, to put it crudely, not be above twelve words or so long. Admittedly, even some of the prohibitions of the Decalogue are longer than this; but not the ones that are always being quoted.

I am not against these simple principles as guides; indeed, it is very important to have them if we are not going to succumb to all kinds of temptations and special pleadings; but all the same I have some sympathy with the 'amoralist'. He looks at the complexities of the world as we actually find it, and at the changes that are constantly occurring in our environment – changes often undreamt of by those who first formulated these simple rules – and it becomes only too obvious to him that to observe these rules always would lead us to do things such that, when we reflect upon them in the light of particular cases which either do or could occur, we cannot possibly approve of them. There thus arises a demand for the justification of these general rules – a demand which their advocates are not able to meet. Moral philosophers have throughout the centuries been trying to satisfy it, and nearly everyone thinks that they have failed. So inevitably the 'amoralist' asks, 'Why have moral rules at all ?'

It is in the context of moral education that the problem is most acute. We constantly hear parents complaining of the amoralism of their children. This is nothing new; it has been going on at least since Socrates' day. But perhaps the problem makes itself felt most acutely at times like the present, when education, and therefore sophistication, is relatively widespread. The parents – let us face it – are on the losing side. They have themselves acquired (who knows how ?) these moral rules, and they pay at least lip-service to them. But when it comes to justifying them they are at a loss. They try to pass on to their children the habit of obedience to these rules; but as soon as their children reach the age at which they begin to think morally (though probably they do not call it 'morally') for themselves, they start questioning the rules, and a certain rising percentage of them, finding no justification which convinces them, will not merely reject particular items from among them, but throw over the whole enterprise of 'morality' (as they call it) altogether. And there is nothing much the parents can do about this. For it is inherent in the parent–child relation that both parties to it are growing steadily older, and the balance of power is thus inexorably shifting. In this argument, the children are certainly going to have the last word. The only weapon the parent has is moral education; and this he is quite unable to wield, because he does not know what morality is, and therefore has no idea what he is trying to inculcate.

I have often heard moral philosophers reproached for doing nothing to remedy this situation; and the reproach is justified. So let us consider two different ways in which as moral philosophers we might try to help. The first way is that which has been advocated, at any rate implicitly, by the kind of moral philosophers whom I am calling descriptivists, who have always throughout the history of the subject been in the majority, and are still prevalent in all the main philosophical schools. The second is that which I myself think more helpful.

What the descriptivist thinks is needed is a way of proving to the young – or at least of getting them to agree – that the things that have been thought right and wrong up to now are, in fact, right and wrong. Once the young have accepted this, they will behave as they should. The two most popular kinds of descriptivism have been the kinds that are conveniently labelled intuitionism and naturalism – though philosophers are so sophisticated nowadays that it would be hard to tie either of these '-ism'-labels to any well-trained modern philosopher with assurance. Both kinds of descriptivism treat moral judgements as statements of fact differing, as regards their factuality, not at all from any other statements of fact. I am, I know, speaking now in a most unprofessionally and indeed unprofessorially crude way. Their purpose is to enable us to say to those who are in moral perplexity, and also to those who doubt or reject the standard moral rules, that these rules have a status like, for example, the fact that ice is lighter than water or even the fact that seven and five make twelve. We can, they think, ascertain the truth of moral statements without doing anything beyond making ourselves conversant with the meanings of the moral words and then using our faculties. The intuitionist thinks that we can ascertain these moral facts directly by the exercise of a special faculty called moral intuition. The naturalist thinks that we can ascertain them indirectly; once we understand properly the meanings of the moral words, we shall see that moral judgements are either equivalent to, or at least entailed by, certain statements of empirical fact; and the truth of these latter we can ascertain in the ordinary way. I have, as I said, put these positions extremely crudely, and I am sure that in this crude form nobody in my audience is going to admit that he holds either of them; but I have not myself found the refinements upon them which have been elaborated any more helpful than the crude versions – only more elusive. So I shall speak about the crude versions, in the assurance that what I say about them will apply, given a few more twists, to their more subtle modern developments.

I am not going to rehearse the well-known arguments against intuitionism and naturalism at the theoretical level; I have done it before, and others have done it better, and I have nothing to add. What I am going to do is to show that, even if intuitionism or naturalism or other forms of descriptivism were theoretically unimpeachable, they would still utterly fail to produce the practical results which are expected of them. We may admit for the sake of argument that there is a sense of moral judgements in which we can ascertain their truth by exercising a faculty for which 'moral intuition' might be a possible name; or we may admit that there is a sense of moral judgements in which they really do follow analytically from certain statements of empirical fact. But if this is the sense of moral judgements that we are going to teach the young, we shall be having no effect upon their conduct.

Let us suppose that we read in the newspaper that, as happens from time to time, some young men have, just for kicks, unscrewed a section of railway line in the middle of a tunnel, or the like. We can quite easily teach the young – even those young men themselves who do these things – that it is wrong to do this sort of thing, provided that we are using a sense of 'wrong' in which our demonstrations work. And they will work if it is either the case that this sense of 'wrong' makes it analytic to say that the gratuitous endangering of life is wrong, or that the feeling of revulsion which all normally educated people have when they contemplate such acts is itself a sufficient indication that the acts are wrong. But what shall we have gained if we get everyone to agree that in one of these senses of 'wrong' the acts are wrong? As I said, even the criminals themselves may admit this. But in admitting this, they will only have been admitting a fact without any essential bearing on their conduct. They can readily allow that the act does arouse the familiar feeling of revulsion; but they may say that they find this feeling of revulsion, and the thought that everyone

who reads about their act in the newspapers will experience it,
exciting – that is just what attracts them about the act. It is
perhaps the knowledge that the act is wrong in this sense that
makes it worth doing. Or they may agree that to endanger the
lives of a trainload of people is wrong – indeed, if they have
learnt some philosophy, they may agree that it is analytic to
say that it is wrong – in perhaps the only sense of 'wrong' with
which they are familiar, its descriptive sense. But this is also a
sense in which one can quite easily say, 'Wrong: so what?'
And that is what they will say.

So if we were following the descriptivists of either sort in our
moral education, we should have taught the next generation a
use of the moral words in which it was tolerably easy to establish that certain acts are right or wrong, but in which the
knowledge that they were right or wrong would be without any
necessary bearing on people's conduct. Indeed, that is what
many well-meaning parents, abetted by many well-meaning
clergymen, schoolmasters and even moral philosophers, have
already succeeded in doing. Their children and pupils know
perfectly well that all sorts of things, from growing their hair
long to extra-marital sex and to murder, are wrong; but they
do not see that that is any reason for abstaining from them.
They have, as in Kierkegaard's fable,[1] mistaken the wig for the
man. There is something very pathetic about these descriptivist
families, of whom I have been acquainted with many; having
quite failed to diagnose the disease which afflicts them, they
often come to moral philosophers for more of the same useless
remedy.

But what is the disease which afflicts them ? Simply that they
have never learnt that the only sense of moral words which
matters in the moral life is their prescriptive sense. There is a
sense of 'wrong' in which to think that an act is wrong is *eo ipso*
to be disposed to refrain from doing it – a sense, even, in which
if you think it wrong you *will* refrain from doing it unless you
succumb to irresistible temptation. If we could teach people to
use 'wrong' in this sense, we should have at least achieved the
object of ensuring that, so far as in them lay, they would refrain
from what they thought wrong. But we should have done this
at a cost: the cost of not predetermining the content of their
moral judgements. No moral judgements of substance can, in

[1] *Concluding Unscientific Postscript*, s.f.

this sense of the moral words, be passed off as analytic, or self-evident. This amounts to saying that, in teaching them to use the moral words in this way, we are tying their actions to their moral judgements, but setting them free to make their own moral judgements. What I am urging is that this cost has to be accepted, if morality is to survive. For although all of us have to go through a stage (sometimes called the stage of heteronomy) in which we get our moral judgements made for us, we have, if we are going to grow up morally, to reach the stage at which we make them for ourselves.

But, it may be asked, what guarantee is there that, once set free, they will not prescribe universally that people should cause train-crashes if they find it exciting ? Simply that if they did this they would be prescribing that they themselves should be thus endangered by anybody who found it exciting, if and when they travel in trains. Of course they may not think of this, for people are often thoughtless. But the problem of making them think about the consequences of their actions for other people – of what it is like to be in the situations in which they are putting other people – is not a philosophical one. If anybody does give sufficient thought and imagination to the situations of the other people with whom he comes into contact, and treats them as if it were he that was in those situations, he will not prescribe universally that people should cause train-crashes in tunnels for fun unless he himself genuinely wants this to be done, even when he is a passenger. Indeed, not even this is enough; for he has to want it to be done, even when he is a passenger *and* wants there not to be a crash as much as the passengers in this train, which he is causing to crash, want there not to be a crash.

I am not pretending that philosophy can solve all the problems of moral education. That would be pressing the claims of my subject too far. I am claiming only that it can remove one serious obstacle to success, namely ignorance of what we are trying to achieve. If once we understand what morality is – that it is not the same thing as conformity, but is the endeavour of a free agent to find for himself principles which he can accept as binding on all alike – then we shall be on the way to solving the many problems which remain. We are trying to educate people so that they, first of all, think about, and are able to assess reliably, the consequences of their actions for other people. So, although moral judgements are not, in the narrow

sense, statements of fact, knowledge of the facts is of over-
whelming importance in moral thinking; it is safe to say that
by far the greatest number of people slip up in their moral
thinking through ignorance or neglect of the facts. But secondly,
they have to give as much weight to the interests of these other
people as to their own interests; for unless they do this, they
will not be universalising their prescriptions. To say that sole
(or even preponderant) weight should be given to my interests
just because they are mine is to utter a prescription which in
principle defies universalisation. For to say that I should give
sole weight to everybody's interests just because they are his
is to contradict myself. It is logically impossible to give most-
favoured treatment to everybody. To say, on the other hand,
that *everybody* should give sole weight to *his own* interests, just
because they are his, is, indeed, to utter a self-consistent universal prescription; but it is one which hardly anybody is going to
accept once he has considered the effects which compliance
with it by others would have on his own interests. For he would
be implicitly prescribing to others to put him in the cooler. If
he really thinks this, he must desire, or at any rate be content,
that they should put him in the cooler – provided only that he
realises the undoubted fact that to put him in the cooler is in
the interests of nearly everybody with whom he comes in
contact, if he is really prescribing and following a principle of
complete neglect of other people's interests.

Let us, without claiming historical accuracy, call this last
position the Nietzschean position, and admit that it is logically
self-consistent; but let us add, since this is intended as a practical
lecture, that Nietzscheans are not likely to trouble us in practice,
any more than the other two kinds of logically possible eccen-
trics that I mentioned earlier. There will be plenty who err
through ignorance or neglect of the facts; and there are non-
philosophical disciplines whose business it is to put them right.
There will also be plenty who are insensitive or lacking in
imagination; literature and drama can perhaps do something
for the education of these – but the character of their human
environment in their families and schools is more important.
Others are suffering from psychological defects, such that they
cannot be brought to attend to the facts, or to other people as
people like themselves, or to think clearly what they are saying
or doing. The psychologists can, perhaps, find out eventually

7 The Argument from Received Opinion

I aim in this paper to clarify, if I can, the logic of a form of argument that has been exceedingly common in moral philosophy. Socrates' argument against the first proffered definition of justice in the first book of the *Republic* has usually been taken to be an example of this form of argument: 'Everybody would say that *p*; but on your theory it would be false that *p*; so the theory must be wrong.' So also has Aristotle's argument for the view that pleasure is a good in the *Nicomachean Ethics* (1172 b36): 'What everybody thinks, that, we say, is the case; one who does away with this reliance will not, you may be sure, say anything more reliable.' There are other possible interpretations of Plato's and Aristotle's arguments, one of which I shall shortly suggest; and it would be good if they were correct, for the interpretations which I have just given make the arguments open to serious objection. But the melancholy truth is probably that neither Plato nor Aristotle had the logical equipment which would have enabled them to distinguish between the different interpretations. Since the equipment was not invented until many centuries later, this is neither culpable nor surprising.

There is less excuse for more recent philosophers who have been confused on this point; and although I do not wish to attribute the confusion to anybody in particular, I think that if philosophers generally were clearer about some distinctions which I am shortly going to make, the discussions between, for example, the utilitarians and their deontologist opponents might have proved a great deal more illuminating than they actually have. These arguments have often taken the following form. Utilitarians have put forward as a supreme moral principle one of the many varieties of their type of theory. Their opponents have then pointed out that, in particular cases which they describe, this principle would commit its adherents to moral

views which are very much at variance with those of most
people.

It has usually been held that a point has been scored by this
move. Indeed, the main attraction of rule-utilitarianism has
been that it was thought to be immune to this kind of objection.
But it has remained utterly unclear why the argument should
be thought to have any force. After all, some received opinions
(for example, that it is intrinsically wrong for men and women
to bathe in each others' company) have been abandoned just
because no utilitarian justification could be given for them;
people said 'What harm does it do?', and, after enough people
had said this, the practice came to be generally approved.

In many of the current arguments about medical practices,
the utilitarian standpoint is thought to have consequences which
are shocking (for example, it is thought that the arguments
which are brought forward for abortion in certain cases would
also justify infanticide in similar cases); how are we to tell
whether this shocked reaction ought to be treated like that of
those who objected to mixed bathing, or whether in this case,
but not in that, currently received opinion ought to be treated
as authoritative? Unless we are going to say – and I do not
think that many people would say this – that, in Aristotle's
phrase (as interpreted above), 'what everybody says, is the
case', we shall have either to reject received opinion altogether
as an authority, or find some way of distinguishing between
those opinions of the many which we ought to accept as the
basis of arguments in moral philosophy, and those which we
may legitimately reject when our philosophical reflections have
cast doubt on them. But I do not think that any at all satisfactory way of deciding this question has yet been suggested.

The crucial distinction which has to be made is one which was
perhaps not *clearly* made before Moore; and even he, although
he made it very clearly, did not sufficiently explore its basis.
This is the distinction between the questions 'What things are
good?' and 'What does "good" mean?' (*Principia Ethica*, pp.
3 ff.). The distinction can, indeed, be extracted from many of
the remarks of the Platonic Socrates; but it never becomes
entirely clear in either Plato or Aristotle. This is because they
lacked a clear distinction between analytic and synthetic
truths, or even between first-order and metalinguistic enquiries;

the word 'necessity', as they used it, covered both analytic and synthetic necessity. That is why it is so hard, in both writers, to tell whether the question 'What is the good ?' is a request for the analysis of a concept or for a substantial value-judgement of a very fundamental kind – in Moore's terms, whether what is wanted is an answer to the question 'What does "good" mean ?' or to the question 'What thing is (pre-eminently) good ?' But it would be outside the scope of this paper to justify these remarks.

For 'good' here we could substitute any other moral (or for that matter evaluative) word, and the distinction would still remain crucial. Many have thought (Moore probably among them) that it would remain crucial *whatever* word, evaluative or descriptive, we substituted for 'good'; and in a sense this is true. But I shall be concerned with the consequences of the distinction for ethics; and in ethics the failure to observe it is peculiarly damaging.

It will be instructive to explore the reasons for this. In the case of descriptive predicates, once we have learnt their meaning, we have learnt to what sorts of things they are properly applied. If a man, confronted with a triangle in normal circumstances, said that it was not triangular, we should take this as a sign that he had not learnt the meaning of the word 'triangular'. This (the fact that to know the meaning is to be able to recognise the proper application) might be treated as a defining property of the expression 'descriptive predicate'. On the other hand, what I have just said is true of evaluative words only if we assimilate them in this respect to descriptive words. Many respected philosophers have done just this; but I do not wish to follow them, for the very reason that to do so would commit me to accepting received opinion as authoritative – as we shall see. I wish, on the contrary, to be able to say 'Everybody else, I admit, says that such and such a practice is right, but in my view it is not', without being open to the objection to which I should be open if I did this with the word 'triangular' – the objection that I cannot have learnt the correct meaning of 'right'. If I had lived in fifth-century Athens, and had been very much in advance of my time, the practice in question might have been slavery. I wish, therefore, to insist at any rate in the case of moral words that I can be using such words correctly, and in accordance with their general current use, although the moral opinions which I use them to express differ from those of other people, however numerous. In order to retain this liberty, I need to be able to distinguish between *the current use of the moral words* (which I may not wish to question) and *the current moral opinions* (which I may wish very much to question).

This is what makes Moore's distinction so much more important in the case of evaluative words than it is in the case of descriptive words. For although in the 'triangular' case there is certainly a distinction between the questions 'What does "triangular" mean?' and 'What things are triangular?', in this case to learn the answer to the first question is to acquire an objection-proof method of answering the second; if I know the meaning of 'triangular', I know that all I have to do to determine whether I have a triangular figure in front of me is to determine whether what is in front of me is a plane rectilinear figure with just three sides. But if anybody thought that the same sort of thing could be done in the case of moral words, and then found himself at variance with the general public about what things were right or wrong, he would be in a difficulty. For he would have to admit, either that he was using the words in the same sense as the general public, but was just mistaken in his moral opinions, or else that his use of the words was eccentric. I am assuming that the non-moral facts are known.

In either case he would have no alternative but to accept the moral opinions of the general public; for he would, in either case, have to admit that in its sense (the current one) the general public was correct in its opinions. For if the current senses of the words 'right' and 'wrong' could be captured in a descriptive definition similar to that of 'triangular', then the things which the general public, using its definition, identified as right and wrong would *be* right and wrong (in that sense), unless the general public misapplied the definition, which we may assume not to be the case. It is true that our eccentric could go on disagreeing *verbally* with the general public by having a private definition of 'right' and 'wrong' and sticking to it. But what good would this do him if he had, all the same, to agree in substance with the general public that in its senses of the words what it thought was right *was* right, and what it thought wrong *was* wrong? In any case, we can hardly think that moral reformers who disagree with the general public are indulging in a merely verbal disagreement. The fact is that they are in agreement with the general public about the meanings of the words; they are using them in the *same* way in order to express *different* moral opinions – a situation which would be impossible if the words were descriptive words like 'triangular'.

Having said a little (though not enough) about this crucial distinction between the questions 'What do "right" and "wrong" mean ?' and 'What things are right and wrong ?', and about the consequential distinction between the questions 'In what senses do people use the words "right" and "wrong" ?' and 'What things do people think are right and wrong ?', let me now try to use these distinctions to shed light on our problem. The problem was one of how to tell when, if ever, the appeal to received opinion against the moral views of philosophers is compelling.

After what I have said, it will be obvious that, besides the interpretation which I gave of Plato's and Aristotle's arguments, another is possible. Indeed, there are several different alternatives in Aristotle's case, and I shall not attempt to examine them here. But in the Plato passage it is obvious that the argument would be a great deal more cogent if, instead of depending upon the acceptance of common moral opinion about what is right or just, it depended only on the commonly accepted use of these words. It should by now be clear that these different bases for the argument have to be distinguished, though it is doubtful whether Plato distinguished them.

In its new form the argument would run as follows: 'Everyone would say that *p*; but on your definition it would be *self-contradictory* to say that *p*; so the definition must be wrong.' This form of argument certainly looks a great deal more cogent than the one given earlier, which ran: 'Everyone would say that *p*; but on your theory it would be *false* that *p*; so the theory must be wrong.' For it is much more difficult to suppose that everyone goes about uttering self-contradictory statements than it is to suppose that everyone goes about uttering false ones. Leaving on one side questions about the sense in which moral judgements can be called 'true' or 'false', we feel on much firmer ground if we take the ordinary use of words as authoritative, and therefore refuse to admit a definition which would make the statements of ordinary people self-contradictory, than if we take common moral opinions as authoritative, and refuse to admit

I

a theory which would make them false. To revert to the examples already given: if everyone says that slavery is right, it does not in the least follow that it is right; but if everyone (to use Plato's own example) says that it would be wrong to give a madman back his weapons, any definition which would make it self-contradictory to say this does take a bit of swallowing.

I will now propound the thesis which it is the purpose of this paper to argue. Common moral opinions have in themselves no probative force whatever in moral philosophy (either in theoretical ethics, which is concerned with the meanings of the moral words, or in normative ethics, or morals, which is concerned with the principles of conduct). They appear to have probative force, and have been treated as if they had it, because of a failure to observe the distinctions which I have been making. What does have probative force (directly in theoretical ethics, and only indirectly, and with the help of other factors, in morals) is the ordinary use of the moral words.

Since, however, the positive part of the thesis will be misunderstood, I must add an explanation. I am putting forward only a very modest thesis, which I think would be accepted by nearly everybody. It is that if we are trying to explain the meanings of the moral words as they are used, the way they are used is authoritative for the correctness or incorrectness of our account. If we say that the words are used in a way in which they are not, then we are just wrong. It is, of course, open to us to propose that they be used in a different way, provided that we make clear that this is what we are doing. But even if we do this there is a danger to be avoided. It is sometimes suggested that, for example, a naturalist could escape Moore's refutation or some version of it by putting his theory in the form of a *proposal* that the moral words should be used in accordance with his new naturalistic definition. The objection to this move is that the moral problems which trouble ordinary people are posed in terms of the words as they are ordinarily used: those are the questions that are being asked. It is therefore beside the point to propose definitions which, if they were adopted, would enable different questions to be asked which might be more easily answerable (for example, by showing that some particular answers to them are analytically true, according to the proposed definition). Such a procedure would leave the moral problems of the ordinary man untouched – though he might be, by a philosophical trick, deceived into thinking that the new questions were what he had really been asking all the time. But if the old questions were important ones, such a deception could be only temporary.

We must also be clear (in accordance with our distinction between common moral opinions and the common use of the moral words) that when I say that the common use is authoritative, I am not saying that it is authoritative for any substantial question of morals. If, indeed, a naturalistic definition of some moral word were a correct account of its common use, then from this common use there would follow substantial conclusions about moral questions – and this, in fact, is just why naturalistic definitions are unacceptable, as I said above. But if, as I think, the common use of moral words does not, by itself, commit us to any substantial moral conclusions, it is in principle possible to say that we regard the common use as authoritative for an analysis of that use, but do not regard common moral opinions as authoritative for substantial questions of morality. The words mean what people use them to mean, but that does not by itself stop us rejecting the opinions which are expressed in those words, even if (as assumed above) the non-moral facts are known to all.

It is, no doubt, a misunderstanding on this point that makes some people antipathetic to any reference to 'the ordinary uses of words' in moral philosophy: they think that, if they allow such an 'appeal to ordinary language', they will find themselves committed to ordinarily received opinions about moral questions of substance. And this is what will indeed happen, if any form of naturalism is accepted which establishes its definitions of moral terms by an appeal to common use. But this danger is avoided if, while ready to accept ordinary people as arbiters on the question of what they mean by moral terms, we find (as we certainly shall find if we carry out our investigations properly) that what they do mean by them is nothing that could be captured by a naturalistic definition. For then, in accepting an account of what people mean by these terms which is based on a careful study of how they use them, we shall not at the same time be committing ourselves to the moral opinions which people use them to express.

It may help to illustrate this point if I take as an example a simple, though undoubtedly false, theory of what 'wrong' means which brings out very clearly the distinction which I have been labouring. Suppose that it were established that what ordinary people mean by 'That is wrong' is 'Do not do that'. The acceptance of this (no doubt false) imperativist theory of what the word 'wrong' means in the mouth of ordinary people would not in the slightest commit us to accepting the prohibitions which ordinary people express (according to the theory) by using the word 'wrong'. For we could be in complete agreement with ordinary people in our use of the word 'wrong', and yet utterly reject all the prohibitions on which ordinary people were agreed. For example, if ordinary people thought mixed bathing wrong, we could, while still using the word 'wrong' in the same way, hold that there was nothing wrong with mixed bathing. On this imperativist analysis, we should be withholding, and ordinary people would be issuing, the same command, in the same sense, 'Do not bathe in the company of members of the other sex'. Although, as I have said, the theory which I have used as an example is undoubtedly false, the same possibility of agreement in use coupled with disagreement in moral opinion is open on other, and perhaps more tenable, theories such as my own.

It is also possible for us to have meaningful and unambiguous communication with ordinary people (i.e. not to be at cross-purposes with them), since we and they are using the words in the same senses, even though we are in substantial disagreement. The same possibility of communication between people with different moral opinions is open generally – not only in the no doubt rare case in which a few people are at variance with the unanimous opinion of all their contemporaries, but in the much commoner case in which there are a number of opinions on a given question, each of which has a respectably large group of supporters. On such a theory, unlike naturalism, these groups are able to discuss their differences with one another, agreeing in their use of the words, though they disagree on the substantial questions.

I said earlier that common moral opinions have in themselves no probative force whatever in moral philosophy. I must now try to explain why, if so, they have been so often appealed to by moral philosophers. Are these moral philosophers merely being conservative or conventionally-minded or just stupid ? Or is there really a good argument, or several good arguments, lying concealed behind this bad one which I am calling the argument from received opinion ? I shall argue that there are at least two.

The first good argument is an argument in theoretical ethics which I have already discussed. If someone is purporting to analyse the ordinary use of moral terms, and can be shown to be, by the analysis which he advocates, making ordinary people's opinions self-contradictory, then, unless he can defend himself by explaining how it is that people can contradict themselves in this way without noticing it, his analysis can hardly be right. And an extension is possible to this argument which gives it greater application. What if the analysis which is being advocated makes the opinions of ordinary people, not indeed self-contradictory, but such that it is very strange that they should hold them ? Or, putting it the other way round, it is a strong point in favour of an ethical theory if it enables a natural and readily acceptable explanation to be given of why people hold the moral opinions that they do, given that that is what they mean by them. It is one of the virtues of Hume's approach to ethics that, having explained to the best of his ability what people mean by the moral judgements that they make, he goes on to say why, being the sort of people that they are, it is natural that they should arrive at the moral principles which nearly all of us accept. The ethical theory is tested, in conjunction with certain hypotheses about human nature, by seeing whether in fact human beings, or most of them, do accept the moral principles that we should expect them to accept if they have the natural characteristics that they have and mean by the moral principles what the theory says they mean.

I do not agree with Hume's ethical theory; but it is incumbent on anybody who advances an ethical theory (that is to say, a theory about what the moral words mean) to test it in the same way. I may perhaps be allowed to illustrate this by asking how the test would apply to my own theory. This is, that moral judgements are universal or universalisable prescriptions, permissions or prohibitions. We have therefore, in order to test the theory, to ask whether we should expect people, being the sort of creatures that we think they are, to adopt just those universal prescriptions, etc., that we do as a matter of fact find them adopting. Without applying the test exhaustively, I will illustrate its application by a simple example. Why is it that we find that nearly all societies have a moral principle which forbids gratuitous killing of other people? According to the theory, to ask this is to ask why nearly all societies accept a universal prohibition on gratuitous killing of other people. And the answer is not difficult to give: hardly anybody wants to be killed; if the killing is gratuitous, and if therefore there is no desire of any other person that is satisfied by it, we can all readily accept a prohibition on such killing, since, when we universalise the prohibition, putting ourselves in the place of each of the parties involved, we do not find that any of our desires are thereby frustrated; but when we put ourselves in the place of one of the parties in particular (the victim) we find that our very important desire to stay alive is frustrated by the act, and thus protected by the prohibition on the act.

It would take us too far away from our problem to apply the same kind of test to the more complicated case of the prohibition which most of us accept on non-gratuitous killings of certain kinds; I will be bold enough to claim that the application, in this way, of a theory of the type which I advocate to the various kinds of homicide will enable us to sort out in an acceptable way those which are culpable from those which are not. We shall do this by asking what universal prescriptions, permissions and prohibitions we can accept for certain specified sorts of case, and we shall answer this question by putting ourselves in the places of each of the parties affected and accepting those prescriptions, etc., which will preserve their interests as far as possible. We shall thus (proceeding from Kant to Mill) use some form of utilitarian calculation; but it is beyond the scope of this paper to ask what form.

So then, one of the ways in which the examination of the moral opinions of ordinary people can help the moral philosopher is by providing a test of the adequacy of his theories about the meanings of the moral words, and thus of their logical properties and the arguments which they generate. It must be emphasised again that this procedure in no way commits us to accepting the moral opinions themselves. A utilitarian therefore, of whatever sort, remains at liberty, while agreeing with the ordinary man's use of the moral words, to use them in this very same way to express opinions at variance with those of the ordinary man. To take an example which we have used already: if at some period the ordinary man thinks that mixed bathing is wrong, the utilitarian who does not think this and therefore says that it is not wrong may still be using the word 'wrong' in the same sense as the ordinary man, and the ethical theory about the analysis of the word which he holds may admit this quite explicitly, without convicting himself of inconsistency. It must be understood that utilitarianism is itself a normative view, not an analytical ethical theory, and can therefore be combined with a variety of such analytical theories.

Only, if the utilitarian disagrees with the ordinary man in substance while agreeing with him in the use of words, he is under an obligation to explain how it is that he and the ordinary man come to their different opinions. In the mixed bathing case this may be quite easy. The ordinary man in the early twentieth century thought that mixed bathing was wrong simply because that view had been effectively preached to him from his earliest years; on the other hand, the utilitarian may think that there is nothing wrong in it because he has thought the question out in the way described above, putting himself in the place of all those affected, and decided that he can best serve their interests by rejecting the prohibition on mixed bathing, because, as he says, it does nobody any harm. On this question of mixed bathing, as a matter of historical fact, utilitarians engaged in moral discussion with the ordinary man and converted him, using the moral words in the same senses as he was using them throughout, so that the ordinary man too now thinks that there is no harm, and therefore nothing wrong, in mixed bathing. Perhaps they will have the same success in the matter of bathing with no clothes on, unless the vendors of ten-guinea bikinis continue to convince the ordinary man by advertising that these are even more felicific than nakedness.

There are other cases in which the utilitarian can convert the ordinary man by actually getting him to change his desires, and therefore what he thinks of as harm. Suppose that the general public sees nothing wrong in discarding litter all over the countryside, because it does not mind looking at litter. A few enthusiastic utilitarian conservationists may in the end get all their fellow-citizens to prefer their beauty-spots without cigarette-packets scattered on the grass; and they may then begin to reprobate those who leave them there. We should be unlikely to be persuaded by a moral philosopher that the conservationists, at the start of their campaign, must have been mistaken in thinking that it was wrong to leave litter about, because this view was at variance with the almost unanimous opinion of mankind.

However, not all disputes between the utilitarian and the ordinary man have such a happy ending for the utilitarian. Other cases may convince us that it is not merely the moral language of the ordinary man that deserves to be respected, but also his opinions themselves; although these have no probative force, a proper attention to them may make us revise, not our ethical (i.e. analytical) theory as in the first type of 'good argument', but our normative moral principles; we may come to think either that the form of utilitarianism which we have embraced is inadequate and needs revision (which was what those utilitarians thought who abandoned act-utilitarianism in favour of rule-utilitarianism), or that, though the form of utilitarianism was all right, we had not applied it correctly to the particular case in question. We may say this because, very often, many heads are better than one, and many ordinary men in the course of generations may have seen aspects of the question which in our relatively brief experience we have ignored.

To illustrate this second way in which the moral philosopher can be helped by considering the opinions of the ordinary man, let us take a well-known case from the literature – that of the six people pushing the stalled car over the brow of the hill to start it.[1] It has been alleged by anti-utilitarians that one of the party could reason as follows: 'If five of us push, the car will get over the hill; so it is optimific if one of us merely pretends to push; everybody else is too stupid or too honest to take advantage of this reasoning and only pretend to push; so I ought to be the one who does this, because the rule to do precisely that

[1] See D. Lyons, *Forms and Limits of Utilitarianism*, pp. 128 ff., and G. Ezorsky, *J. Phil.*, LXV (1968) 536 ff. Another well-known case, that of the death-bed promise, is discussed on somewhat similar lines in my *Freedom and Reason*, pp. 132 ff. In the same chapter I show, in a way not unlike Lyons's more intricate discussion, the difficulty of distinguishing act- from rule-utilitarianism; and I shall therefore not attempt here to distinguish them.

in precisely this situation is the rule whose observance would maximise utility.' There are, as anybody knows who has pushed cars, a good many implausibilities in this story; to make it serve the argument we have to ignore the possibility that they might all push, but not quite so hard, or draw lots to decide who should be the one to take a rest.

Anti-utilitarians might argue that the ordinary man would disagree strongly with the utilitarian reasoning which I have just set out, and that therefore the reasoning, and with it the type of utilitarian theory on which it is based, must be rejected. So far this is just an argument from received opinion, and has no more value than the similar arguments about litter, slavery and mixed bathing. It is indeed likely that more of us, here and now, will be moved by the argument in the car-pushing case than in the others; but that may be merely because in the car-pushing case more of us share, initially, the opinions of the ordinary man and therefore have a prejudice against any view which would require us to abandon them. The utilitarian could retort that apart from this contingent prejudice there is no difference between the cases.

What is needed to establish a difference is an analysis of the argument in all of them to show – if it can be shown – that in the other cases there is no good reason for the opinions of the ordinary man, but only a historical explanation, whereas in the car-pushing case there is a good reason. I shall not attempt the first half of this task, though I think it could be performed; but I will try to show that in the car-pushing case the ordinary man is being perfectly rational, even on an appropriately formulated utilitarian view. I owe here a debt to Professor Gertrude Ezorsky (loc. cit.), though the formulation of the argument is quite different from hers; whether what I am producing is, as she calls her article, a 'defense of rule-utilitarianism' depends on the rather unimportant question of what we count as a kind of rule-utilitarianism.

The argument is most simply introduced in terms of my own theory. The person who is contemplating the dastardly act of merely pretending to push has to ask himself whether he is prepared to permit universally that people should, in precisely his situation, act in this way; and he has to ask this, bearing in mind that he might logically be in the situation of any one of the other parties, and therefore not giving greater weight to the interests of any one of them than to that of any other. If he puts the question to himself in this way, he will surely come to the conclusion that he ought to do his bit and push; for if he does not, the interests of each of the others will be harmed, and the total of these harms is much greater than the good that he will do himself by not pushing. I have now, via my own theory, reached what is a recognisably utilitarian form of argument, relying on the Benthamite requirement to count everybody as one, whose basis can only be some form of universalism.

It will, however, be at once objected that I have assumed quite illegitimately that the interests of the others are harmed, and that the total of these harms adds up to more (if such a summation makes sense) than the harm suffered by the defaulter if he had really pushed. This, then, is what I have to establish. It might be thought that, since none of the others knows that the defaulter is not pushing, their interests are not harmed, or not enough to counterbalance the harm that he escapes. It is true that they each push a little harder than they would otherwise have done; but we may suppose that the harm from the mere extra pushing does not add up to enough to tip the balance. In any case this is not the factor that moves the ordinary man. What makes him condemn the defaulter is the sheer iniquity of his deceiving his companions in this way – a factor which, it is alleged, cannot appear in the utilitarian's calculations.

But can it not? Is not to be deceived in this way a harm to one's interests, even if one does not discover the deceit? If I am imagining myself in the position of one of these people, while at the same time retaining, as the imaginer but not as the imaginee (if I may so put it), the knowledge that the defaulter is not pushing, do I not think that a dirty trick is being played on me? The point can be made in at least two other ways which avoid making the move (which some have found suspect) of imagining ourselves being somebody else, or the related move of simultaneously having the knowledge as imaginer while imagining ourselves, as imaginee, not having it. Suppose that we are asked whether we are prepared to permit that this trick should be played on us at some time in the future unknown to us. Should we not then refuse indignantly to permit this?

Or suppose that we are informed that it has been played on us at some time in the past; shall we not then be extremely cross with the man who has played it, and perhaps resolve not to engage in allegedly co-operative enterprises with him in the future ? I conclude from all this that, even in the case where a man remains in total ignorance that he is being cheated in this way, his interests are harmed, though in this case without his knowledge. Although it is perfectly true that what the eye does not see, the heart does not grieve at, nevertheless, if my wife is unfaithful to me but I do not hear about it, my interests are still harmed, because something that I very much want not to happen has happened.

The reason why people have not seen this point is that they put the utilitarian theories which they are defending or attacking in terms of present states of feeling such as pleasure and its opposite. They therefore reason that, since the man who is successfully deceived experiences (now and later) no diminution of pleasure or increase of whatever the opposite feeling-state is called, he cannot be being harmed. But a man's interests are harmed not only when his actual feeling-states are adversely affected, but also when desires which he has (for example, not to be cheated) are, even unknown to him, frustrated. And when these harms are added to the total in our example, they may be more than enough to tip the balance in favour of the ordinary man's condemnation.

At this point it may be objected that the desire not to be cheated, whose frustration I claim to be a harm, is a desire which the pure-blooded utilitarian will not have, and will think that other people ought to suppress even if they have it. For the concept of cheating belongs to a moral vocabulary which the utilitarian has rejected; it goes with justice and fairness and all that. The reason, it might be objected, why we feel annoyed at the thought of being cheated is that we are affected by old-fashioned non-utilitarian ideas of justice and rights, which a utilitarian would abandon. The utilitarian, therefore, cannot make use of the argument which I have just set out (it may be thought), because it appeals to notions which he has discarded. In other words, the argument which is used to show that the ordinary man has good reason for objecting to the action of the defaulter is an argument some of whose ingredients are not available to the utilitarian; the utilitarian therefore (it might be said) cannot make use of it in order to show that his system really leads to the same conclusions as are acceptable to common opinion.

But there is an answer to this objection. First of all, the utilitarian has not abandoned notions of justice and fairness. He has incorporated them into his system. The formal principle of justice is nothing other than the requirement, which is the basis of utilitarianism, that everybody is to count as one. It has, no doubt, been disputed whether this formal principle is enough to generate all our common notions of what is just and unjust; but it is open to the utilitarian to claim that each of these notions either can be vindicated by a careful application of his formal principle to the actual situations in which human beings, natured as they are, find themselves; or, if not, ought to be rejected. It would be a huge task to show this generally; but let us attempt it in the particular case which we are considering.

The essence of the objection was that, in the argument as set out, a *moral* notion (that of cheating) was imported which was not available to the utilitarian. The answer to it is that this moral notion is not required for the argument. All that is required is *resentment*. The reason why we (normally) resent somebody else taking a rest while we push for his benefit is not, initially, that we have any moral notions; it is simply that we feel that he has taken advantage of us, and hate him for it. It is a fact of human nature that we experience this feeling – a fact, no doubt, which, when moral forms of thought become current, will result in the content of people's moral opinions being different from what it would have been if they did not have the feeling; but a fact, nevertheless, which would be a fact if moral forms of thought had not been invented.

Given that people have this propensity to feel resentment at other people taking advantage of them, and to desire very strongly that this should not happen, even if they know nothing about it, it will be the case that they are harmed if advantage is taken of them. Thus, in the car-pushing example, if it is the case that (moral notions apart) people very much want not to be in a position, even unwittingly, of pushing cars for the benefit of other people who are only pretending to push, the people who are only pretending to push are harming those who are pushing by causing a state of affairs to obtain which those who are pushing do not want to obtain. When I say that they do not want it to obtain, I do not mean that they are experiencing present feelings of desire; it is sufficient evidence that they want it not to obtain if they would be very annoyed if they discovered that it did obtain – just as it is sufficient that I want my wife to be faithful if I should be very upset if I discovered that she was not.

It must next be asked whether it is regrettable that human nature is as it is in this respect; and whether we ought to try to suppress the dislike we have of being taken advantage of. The utilitarian will be in his element in answering these questions. He will say that it is in fact a very good thing that people who are pushing cars do not like other people, who are getting just as much advantage from the pushing, merely pretending to push. It is a good thing, because the fact that most people dislike this leads to the general reprobation of this kind of deceit, and castigation of those who use it; and this, in turn, leads more people to push than would otherwise push, and so fewer car journeys end abortively. Granted that this particular journey will continue in any case, because the honest men are sufficiently numerous in proportion to the dishonest; yet if the dishonest get away with it, and if there is not a general dislike of having this done to one, it may be predicted that the number of the dishonest will increase disastrously. The utilitarian will therefore argue that this propensity to dislike being taken advantage of should not be suppressed, but positively cultivated, because of the benefits which come from its prevalence in society. No doubt harm also comes from its exercise on improper occasions or with improper objects, or to excess; but which objects and occasions are improper, and how much resentment is too much, ought to be decidable by methods of which the utilitarian could approve.

It is to be noted that in the preceding paragraph I used the word 'general' several times. I used it in the sense in which it *contrasts* with 'universal', in that a proposition can be generally true, but have exceptions, whereas one which is universally true cannot. Writers in this field have often used the word 'general' when what they mean is 'universal'; but this has been a source of confusion. The defaulter in our example has to ask himself (like anybody in a moral dilemma) whether he can prescribe, or permit, *universally* that in precisely similar situations people should act in a precisely similar way. But what stops him permitting that they should only pretend to push is that this would harm most other people, because there is a *general* (not necessarily universal) dislike of having this done to one. If he knew that his companions were all unnaturally unselfish and would not mind in the least even if they caught him, the situation would be altered. But because, as we may presume, he does not know this, the general desire not to be deceived provides him with a reason for refusing to accept a universal principle which permits him to deceive them; for, given this general desire, it is highly probable that he will be harming them and, if he is giving as much weight to their interests as to his own, this will stop him accepting such a principle.

So then we may expect the utilitarian and the ordinary man to agree that the human tendency which results in the reprobation of the defaulter in our example not only exists but ought to be cultivated. Why, then, should they not also agree in the moral judgement of reprobation itself? The way they might both get from the bare non-moral desire not to be taken advantage of to the moral reprobation of the man who does this is not hard to discover. Because nearly everybody wants not to be taken advantage of, nearly everybody is ready to subscribe to a universal prohibition – at least in cases like the one described – on taking advantage of other people. This is exactly analogous to the case I took earlier of killing: because nearly everybody wants not to be killed, they will all readily assent to a prohibition on gratuitous killing.

What then are the conclusions which are to be drawn for our main topic from this extended discussion of the car-pushing example? We introduced it in order to show how, in spite of the fact that the opinions of the ordinary man have in themselves no probative force in moral philosophy, a due respect for them may lead us to understand its problems better. They do not supply an argument; but they make us look for one. In this case the utilitarian and his opponent were both applying the utilitarian principle to the situation in too crude a way; and this led them to think that the principle was at variance with our common notions. The conflict is reconciled by a careful attention to the way in which both the utilitarian and the ordinary man, if they are using the moral words in the way that (according to me) they do use them, would naturally and reasonably be led to the same moral conclusion. Thus both the ethical theory (my own) on which the argument was constructed, and the utilitarian position, are vindicated, without doing violence to common opinion.

In other cases the same examination will lead to a rejection of common opinion – the examination has to be done afresh in each case. What we have achieved, if my argument is correct, is a way of deciding which common opinions are to be rejected and which retained – a way which involves treating these common opinions with enough respect to make the effort to discover how they might, if the ordinary man were philosophically more articulate, be justified. The justification is based, first, on the use of the moral terms in the way that the ordinary man uses them, and on a correct philosophical analysis of this use (which does not by itself commit us to any moral opinions, ordinary or extraordinary); and secondly on an examination of the desires which the ordinary man, natured as he is, tends to have, and thus of the interests that he has and of what actions tend to harm those interests; and thirdly on the application of the first of these things to the second – that is to say, the search for principles which we and the ordinary man can accept and which are expressible in the universal prescriptive language which we and the ordinary man both use for our moral discourse. Only thus can we decide rationally which received opinions to continue to receive. And I offer this as an illustration of the truth that the first step to unravelling moral problems is to understand the language in which they are posed.